S0-AVD-222

the new

COOK IT

IN A

CASSEROLE

M. BARROWS AND COMPANY, INC.

PUBLISHERS, *New York*

the new COOK IT IN A CASSEROLE

Florence Brobeck

Third Printing, June 1961

Published simultaneously in the
Dominion of Canada by
George J. McLeod Limited, Toronto.

Manufactured in the United States of America
by H. Wolff, New York
Designed by Betty Kormusis

contents

casseroles:
better than ever

The original *Cook It in a Casserole* was published as a wartime emergency cookbook. Because of the scarcity of metal, the supply of cooking utensils had dwindled and, while pottery and glass bakers were not especially plentiful, Italian, Spanish, and French earthenware casseroles and Limoges bakers were to be had in restaurant-supply stores where chefs shopped. The then new oven-glass wares were just beginning to dominate the kitchen counters in department stores.

METAL-BASE CASSEROLES

Today, for the recipes and menus in this completely new book of casserole meals, a gratifyingly large choice of baking dishes has become available all over America. Their variety and usefulness, charm and durability contribute to the pleasure of meal-planning and preparation. The old-fashioned "soft" earthenware casseroles and glass baking dishes are still favorites of many cooks.

Others prefer the newer, more widely-useful, metal-base baking wares. These are made of porcelain enamel fused to a heavy steel or cast-iron base, making a baking dish which can be used on direct heat on top of the stove for preliminary sautéing and other first steps in casserole cookery. Then these dishes go into the oven, and finally come to the table—satisfyingly functional as well as decorative. They vary in color, shape, size, and style to match the gayest or the most conservative kitchen and dining-room color schemes—solid-color lemon, orange, seafoam-blue, flame, and green. Some are patterned in deeper blue or green. Some are lined with white, others with contrasting color. They come to our kitchens from Scandinavian, Belgian, Dutch, and American manufacturers. These metal-base wares cook evenly, do not break, are as easy to clean as china, a joy to own and use.

FLAMEPROOF, OVENPROOF, OR FIREPROOF CASSEROLES

Other popular modern baking dishes include England's Royal Worcester ovenproof porcelain in the famous petite marmite cups, au gratin dishes, "pigeon" casseroles, deep oval bakers, soufflé and hot canapé dishes. This ware is gleaming white, decorated with gold or silver luster. And please note that *it is ovenproof, not flameproof*. In the same class is Limoges ware from France, those shallow, delicate-looking, fluted white bakers just right for au gratin and countless other recipes. They are not flameproof.

Like these more delicate English and Limoges bakers, the rough "soft" pottery casseroles from France, Italy, Mexico, South America, and Spain cannot be used on top of the stove. And however interesting their primitive peasant shapes and qualities, these homey casseroles are temperamental. They require watchful care in handling, and thorough cleansing immediately after use to prevent a permanent oily odor from developing. They safely survive high oven temperatures, but like glass casseroles must not be put down while hot on a cool or cold table top, tray, or sink board.

Many, many other casseroles are to be had today in various qualities of earthenware, pottery, and new ovenproof china. Their colors, shapes, and styles are too numerous to describe. Many of them bear the names of famous American potteries. Select them for both usefulness and beauty. Use them according to directions on the label or manufacturers' circular.

Flameproof means the dish can be used on direct top-of-the-stove heat. But the phrase *fireproof* on British-made procelain does not mean that the dish can be used on top-of-the-stove heat—only in the oven. *Ovenproof* also indicates oven cookery only. To avoid breakage, use metal-base bakers when first steps of the recipe call for top-of-the-stove cooking.

CARE AND USE

Wash any casserole immediately after a meal: remove any remaining food, fill dish with warm soapsuds, let soak. Wash, rinse, dry, put away. Do not use steel wool and other abrasives and scouring pads on "soft" pottery (peasant) casseroles; nor are these cleansers needed or recommended for porcelain metal-base bakers.

Don't overload the oven with too many baking dishes at one time. Pans and casseroles should not touch each other, nor should they touch the sides of the oven. Center the food on the oven shelf, or stagger casseroles on the two shelves so that one dish is not directly below another.

MENUS ARE EXTENDABLE

Recipes and menus in the following pages are designed for brunch, luncheon, dinner, supper, and other occasions. But they are adaptable and interchangeable to your own wishes and needs because of the informality and ease of casserole meals. A brunch menu may be just what you want to serve for a candlelight supper at midnight after a good evening of listening to records. A dinner menu, minus its first course and with a more simple dessert, may be what you want to serve your brunch guests on an autumn holiday. Or a simple supper menu, with a fine soup and a more elaborate dessert added, can become a dinner menu for special company.

Many of the recipes specify quick-frozen or canned ingredients, biscuit-mixes, and other semiprepared foods. Your cookery will be timesaving and simplified by introducing these and many other such foods which your favorite stores and markets supply, new ones appearing almost daily now. Also a good neighborhood bakery shop makes life easier for a family cook; Armenian, French, Italian, Mexican, Spanish, Scandinavian, and other foreign grocery stores, markets, and bakeries are inspiration and source for many good ingredients and innovations in the menus. The delicious findings at such grocers and elsewhere enable you to be inventive, to garnish and vary recipes and menus.

WINE IN THE DISH

When I am in doubt about the kind and quality, color and fragrance of a wine I would like to add to a dish, or put on the table, I consult authority. I am fortunate in having for a friend Mr. Peter Greig, who goes all over America as advisor on wines to restaurateurs and others. In making these dishes and planning these menus, where a recipe calls simply for white wine, this specialist recommends an all-round wine, neither sweet nor dry. Such a wine is a Graves from Bordeaux, for example. Or from California, a dry Sauterne. A French Sauternes (with an "s") is always sweet. Or a Rhine wine from Germany, without too much individuality, such as a Liebfraumilch. Or a "Rhine wine" made in New York State.

Where a recipe calls for red wine, it is safest to use a Red Bordeaux from France, such as a Bordeaux Rouge, or a Médoc, or a St. Julien. Or try a red Chianti from Italy, or the rough, flavorsome, inexpensive California Chianti. A Red Burgundy, such as Mâcon, or Beaune, or Pommard is good in those dishes where a particularly rich sauce is to be created. A Red Rhône wine, such as Châteauneuf-du-Pape, is also appropriate.

Some of the recipes call for sherry. The type used should always be a dry sherry unless the recipe definitely states otherwise. It pays in cooking to use a good-quality sherry, that is, one made in Spain. Sherry is a complicated and expensive wine to make. A cheap sherry is seldom authentic and usually unpleasant to taste.

The use of sparkling wines, red or white, in cooking is not only an absurd extravagance but such wines add next to nothing to the flavor of the dish. When your kitchen wine cellar holds only American wines, a good guide is: California for red wines, New York State for white.

WINES ON THE TABLE

Rosé wines, which have become so popular, partly because of their gay color, are better served at the table as an accompaniment to a casserole than added in the cooking. Rosés should always be served well chilled. The best come from France, either from Tavel (Provence), a big-bodied wine quite dry in flavor, or from Anjou, in the west of France; these are lighter bodied with a suspicion of sweetness in the flavor.

Italy provides a light-bodied, dry Rosé also, and from California comes Grenache, quite a tart wine, named after the grape from which it is made.

SOME BASIC SAUCES

WHITE SAUCE

THIN WHITE SAUCE

1 tablespoon butter or margarine
1 tablespoon flour
1 cup milk
¼ teaspoon salt
⅛ teaspoon pepper
1/16 teaspoon paprika

MEDIUM WHITE SAUCE

2 tablespoons butter or margarine
2 tablespoons flour
1 cup milk
¼ teaspoon salt
⅛ teaspoon pepper
1/16 teaspoon paprika

THICK WHITE SAUCE

3 to 4 tablespoons butter or margarine
3 to 4 tablespoons flour
1 cup milk
¼ teaspoon salt
⅛ teaspoon pepper
1/16 teaspoon paprika

The procedure for all is the same. Melt the butter or margarine, add flour, and stir smoothly until blended. Add the milk, a little at a time, stirring, and cook over moderate heat; continue to cook and stir several minutes after sauce boils. Season at the end. Makes one cup sauce.

Vary seasoning of white sauce to suit individual taste and the dish being prepared. For instance, onion salt, celery salt, various herbs may be stirred in as the sauce comes off the heat.

For *Curry Sauce,* called for in various recipes in this book, prepare the simple American version using a white sauce as a base. Stir one or more teaspoons curry seasoning or curry powder into the hot white sauce. Or, preferably, heat the curry powder in a heavy saucepan for three minutes. Stir hot white sauce into the hot curry powder, mix and heat two minutes. (More elaborate curry sauces, called for in preparing curries, are made in the pot with the lamb, beef, or other food being curried. My *Cooking With Curry* gives these variations ad infinitum.)

Custard Sauce, necessary for some of the desserts, is also easily made. Here is one of the most simple and flavorful recipes for it:

3 egg yolks, slightly beaten
¼ cup sugar
⅛ teaspoon salt
1½ cups milk
1 teaspoon vanilla extract
½ teaspoon lemon extract

Mix yolks, sugar, and salt in the top of a double boiler. Stir milk in gradually. Cook mixture over hot water, stirring constantly until thickened and spoon is coated. Remove at once from the heat; set upper part of boiler in a pan of cold water. Beat flavorings in. Let cool slightly. Serve warm, or chilled. 6 servings.

Note: Other flavorings, such as sherry or cognac may be used in place of vanilla and lemon extract.

Dishes marked with a * will be found through the menus. These dishes are listed in the Index, their recipes included in this book.

brunch
is in the oven

BRUNCH APPLES AND OATMEAL

4 eating apples
2 tablespoons brown sugar
1 tablespoon grated lemon peel
1 cup light cream
2 cups cooked oatmeal

Wash apples, core, and pare. Slice thin into small casserole (one-quart); sprinkle with sugar and lemon peel, and cover with cream. Bake, uncovered in moderate oven (375° F.) twenty minutes. Cover apples with oatmeal, return to oven, and bake ten minutes. Serve hot with top milk or cream. 4 servings. To vary, split toasted shredded-wheat biscuits and use in place of oatmeal. Pour two tablespoons honey over biscuits. Bake as described.

For big brunch party, place casserole on warmer at table.

MENU

ORANGE-AND-GRAPEFRUIT JUICE
BRUNCH APPLES AND OATMEAL
CRISP BACON
CINNAMON BUNS
COFFEE

BLUEBERRY PUDDING

1 quart blueberries
1 cup sugar
6 slices bread
1½ cups milk
1 egg yolk
Light brown sugar
Cinnamon

Wash berries; drain. Put in flameproof baking dish (one and one-half quart) with sugar. Boil six minutes. Trim crusts from bread and cut each slice diagonally in half. Let soak ten minutes in milk mixed with beaten yolk. Lay bread on top of berries. Sprinkle slices lightly with sugar and cinnamon. Bake in moderately-hot oven (400° F.) fifteen minutes or until lightly browned. Serve hot, with or without cream. 6 servings.

Or cook berries; then bake in individual dishes.

MENU

OATMEAL WITH BROWN SUGAR AND CREAM
SCRAMBLED EGGS WITH VIENNA SAUSAGES
BUTTERED RAISIN TOAST
BLUEBERRY PUDDING
COFFEE

CODFISH BAKE

4 medium-sized potatoes, boiled
½ teaspoon salt
½ cup butter or margarine
8 quick-frozen codfish cakes
2 cups milk
4 tablespoons buttered crumbs
Freshly-ground pepper

Slice potatoes very thin into buttered baking dish (one and one-half quart). Sprinkle with salt; add dabs of butter or margarine. Place codfish cakes on top of potatoes. Add remaining butter. Pour enough milk over all to barely show at top. Cover with crumbs. Add light sprinkling of pepper. Bake in hot oven (425° F.) twenty minutes, or until browned. 4 to 6 servings.

For Crab-Meat Bake, *use quick-frozen crab cakes.*

MENU

ORANGE JUICE
CORN MUFFINS CURRANT JAM
CODFISH BAKE
BAKED APPLES
COFFEE

EASY CODFISH PIE

1 package quick-frozen cooked codfish balls (20 bite-size)
2 cups hot mashed potatoes
½ cup medium white sauce
½ teaspoon salt
¼ teaspoon pepper
¼ cup buttered crumbs

Heat codfish balls as described on package. Place half of the potatoes in a buttered casserole (one-quart). Cover with codfish balls. Pour white sauce over fish. Add seasonings. Cover with remaining mashed potatoes. Sprinkle thickly with crumbs. Bake in hot oven (425° F.) twenty minutes, or until browned. Serve at once. 4 to 6 servings.

For variation, add a tablespoon each chopped onion and green pepper to white sauce.

MENU

STEWED APRICOTS
EASY CODFISH PIE
HOT SALLY LUNN
GOOSEBERRY JAM
COFFEE

CHEESE CORN PUDDING

1 can (1-pound) cream-style corn
1 cup bread crumbs
1 cup milk
2 tablespoons chopped green pepper
1 teaspoon salt
¼ teaspoon pepper
¼ pound Cheddar cheese
4 slices bacon

Combine corn, crumbs, milk, green pepper, and seasonings. Pour into greased baking dish, ten-by-six-by-two inches. Slice cheese as thin as possible; lay slices on top. Cook bacon until half done. Lay across cheese. Bake in moderate oven (325° F.) one hour and fifteen minutes. 4 to 6 servings.

A versatile dish. Good morning, noon, and night.

MENU

PROSCIUTTO WITH HONEYDEW MELON
CHEESE CORN PUDDING
COFFEECAKE RASPBERRY JAM
COFFEE

BRUNCH CORNED BEEF HASH

3 medium-sized potatoes, boiled
Salt and pepper
½ cup milk
3 tablespoons butter or margarine
½ cup chopped peeled onions
1 can (1-pound) corned beef hash
¼ cup coarse crumbs

Slice potatoes into a buttered shallow baking dish. (One layer in large dish.) Season with salt and pepper; pour milk over; add one tablespoon of butter or margarine in dabs. Sauté onions five minutes in one tablespoon fat. Combine with hash and mix well. Spread hash over potatoes. Dot top with remaining butter or margarine, and sprinkle with crumbs. Bake in moderate oven (375° F.) thirty minutes. 4 or 5 servings.

A man can't ask for more—unless it's more helpings.

MENU

STRAWBERRIES AND PUFFED CEREAL WITH CREAM
BRUNCH CORNED BEEF HASH
HOT CORN STICKS QUINCE JAM
COFFEE

CORNED BEEF HASH RING

2 cans (1-pound) corned beef hash
6 eggs
2 tablespoons butter or margarine
Salt and pepper
1 tablespoon chopped water cress

Pack corned beef hash into greased ring mold. Bake in moderate oven (350° F.) thirty minutes. Unmold on warm serving platter. Fill center with scrambled eggs, garnished with water cress. 6 servings.

For supper dish, fill center with creamed mixed green vegetables.

MENU

BLUEBERRIES AND SHREDDED WHEAT WITH CREAM
CORNED BEEF HASH RING
POPOVERS GRAPE JELLY
COFFEE

HASH-STUFFED BAKED APPLES

8 large baking apples
1 can (1-pound) corned beef hash
1 tablespoon minced peeled onion
1 teaspoon Worcestershire sauce
⅛ teaspoon nutmeg
Salt and pepper
1 cup grated sharp Cheddar cheese

Wash apples; core; scoop out extra pulp, leaving large hollow centers; chop pulp. Pare apples one-third of way down from stem end. Combine chopped pulp with hash, onion, and seasonings; mix well. Fill hollows in apples with hash mixture. Set in baking dish (two-quart). Add hot water to a depth of one-half inch. Bake in moderate oven (350° F.) about thirty-five minutes, or until apples are tender. Top with cheese. Return to oven until cheese melts and browns. Serve at once. 8 servings.

A winter favorite in New England with corn bread or popovers.

MENU

PUFFED RICE, BANANAS, AND CREAM
HASH-STUFFED BAKED APPLES
DATE-AND-NUT MUFFINS BUTTER
COFFEE

BRUNCH CRAB CAKES

2 packages quick-frozen crab cakes (4 cakes in package)
1½ cups medium white sauce
½ teaspoon celery salt
¼ teaspoon white pepper
Juice 1 lemon
1 tablespoon chopped green pepper
1 teaspoon cut chives
3 tablespoons rice flakes (dry cereal)

Place cakes in lightly-greased shallow baking dish. Combine white sauce with seasonings, lemon juice, green pepper, and chives. Mix well. Pour over crab cakes. Top with rice flakes. Bake in moderate oven (350° F.) twenty minutes, until hot and browned. 4 servings.

If crab cakes are large, use one package of four.

MENU

PERSIAN MELON WITH FRESH LIME
BRUNCH CRAB CAKES
TOASTED BRIOCHE
RASPBERRY JAM
LITTLE BLUEBERRY TARTS
COFFEE

BRUNCH BAKED EGGS

4 slices bread
Butter
Anchovy paste
¼ cup gravy or medium white sauce
4 eggs
Salt and pepper
1 tablespoon cut chives

Cut bread in rounds; toast on one side. Butter toasted side generously. Add dab of anchovy paste to each and spread into the butter. Place rounds in small buttered baking dish. Pour gravy or white sauce around them. Break eggs, one at a time, into a saucer and slip each egg onto a toast round. Season egg lightly with salt and pepper; add few chives. Set dish in moderate oven (350° F.) and bake until eggs are cooked, ten to fifteen minutes. Vary by using slice of lightly-browned mush under each egg and add tablespoon of tomato sauce to each when half done. 4 servings.

Good late at night, too, for hungry cardplayers.

MENU

MELON BALLS AND SLICED PEACHES
BRUNCH BAKED EGGS
PRUNE DANISH PASTRY
COFFEE

HAIGAGAN OMELET

(NAZ AND GEORGE MARDIKIAN, SAN FRANCISCO)

1 green pepper, chopped fine
½ medium-sized onion, peeled and chopped fine
4 tablespoons butter or margarine
2 large ripe tomatoes, peeled and cut up
¼ pound salami, chopped fine
½ teaspoon salt
6 eggs

Cook the pepper and onion in the butter or margarine five minutes, or until onion is tender. Add tomatoes, and cook five minutes. Add salami and salt, stir and heat to boiling. Remove from heat. Butter bottom of shallow baking pan or dish (nine-inch square). Beat eggs well, combine with tomato mixture. Pour into pan. Bake in hot oven (450° F.) five to ten minutes, or until eggs are set, and lightly browned. Cut in squares and serve immediately on very hot plates. 4 servings.

Often served at Armenian wedding breakfasts in Fresno.

MENU

WHOLE FRESH STRAWBERRIES AND SLICED ORANGES
POWDERED SUGAR
HAIGAGAN OMELET
BROWN-AND-SERVE FRENCH BREAD SLICED AND BUTTERED
COFFEE

NORWEGIAN EGGS

6 hard-cooked eggs
1 cup medium white sauce
¼ cup heavy cream
¼ teaspoon dry mustard
¼ teaspoon Worcestershire sauce
1 can (3¾-ounce) smoked Norwegian sardines
4 tablespoons buttered crumbs

Slice three eggs into buttered shallow baking dish (one-quart). Mix white sauce with cream, mustard, and Worcestershire. Pour a little sauce over eggs; add layer of drained sardines; pour half of remaining cream sauce over sardines; cover with remaining egg slices. Top with remaining cream sauce; sprinkle with crumbs. Bake in moderate oven (350° F.) twenty minutes. 4 servings.

A luncheon and buffet-supper favorite with green salad.

MENU

CANNED GREEN GAGE PLUMS
NORWEGIAN EGGS
BROWN-AND-SERVE CLOVER ROLLS
APRICOT MARMALADE
CINNAMON DOUGHNUTS
COFFEE

ONION BAKED EGGS

2 Spanish onions, peeled and sliced thin
3 tablespoons butter or margarine
1 teaspoon salt
½ teaspoon pepper
Paprika
4 eggs
3 tablespoons buttered crumbs
2 thin slices Cheddar cheese

Cook onions ten minutes in butter or margarine in small flameproof baking dish. Add salt, pepper, and a little paprika. Break eggs, one at a time into a saucer and slip eggs onto onions. Cover with crumbs. Cut cheese in narrow strips and lay crisscross on top of eggs. Bake uncovered in moderate oven (350° F.) twelve minutes, or until eggs are cooked. 4 servings.

Also a good quickie for unexpected supper guests.

MENU

HALF PINK GRAPEFRUIT
ONION BAKED EGGS
BUTTERED WHOLE-WHEAT TOAST
GINGERBREAD AND APPLESAUCE
COFFEE

SPANISH DRUNKEN EGGS

2 cups cooked Lima beans
Salt and pepper
6 slices bacon
6 eggs
3 tablespoons butter, melted
¼ cup white wine

Drain beans; press through sieve into a shallow buttered baking dish. Season purée with salt and pepper. Cook bacon until almost crisp; drain; lay slices on purée. Break eggs one at a time into saucer and slip on top of bacon. Season with salt and pepper. Mix butter and wine together; sprinkle over eggs. Bake in moderate oven (325° F.) twelve minutes, or until eggs are set and reach desired firmness. 6 servings.

Corn sticks or crisp popovers also good with this.

MENU

BLUEBERRIES AND RICE FLAKES
SPANISH DRUNKEN EGGS
BRAN MUFFINS APPLE BUTTER
FRESH PEARS AND MALAGA GRAPES
COFFEE

HADDIE FOR BRUNCH

1 cup finnan haddie pieces
1 cup light cream
4 hard-cooked eggs, sliced thin
1 tablespoon butter or margarine
¼ teaspoon salt
Paprika
2 tablespoons minced parsley
Toast
Lemon Butter

Cover haddie with cold water, bring to boiling, then lower heat and simmer twenty-five minutes. Drain; rinse. Flake the fish. Combine with cream, eggs, butter or margarine, and salt in shallow baking dish (one-quart). Heat in hot oven (450° F.) until bubbly, about ten minutes. Sprinkle with paprika and parsley. Serve on toast spread with Lemon Butter. 4 servings.

Lemon Butter: Blend 3 tablespoons butter with 2 tablespoons lemon juice and 1 tablespoon grated lemon peel. Spread on toast.

A New England favorite with Sunday late-risers.

MENU

GRAPEFRUIT JUICE
HADDIE FOR BRUNCH
SMALL WHOLE-WHEAT ROLLS, TOASTED
ORANGE MARMALADE
COFFEE

CREAMED HAM ON ENGLISH MUFFINS

2 English muffins
4 tablespoons butter or margarine
3 tablespoons flour
¼ teaspoon pepper
¼ teaspoon celery salt
½ teaspoon Worcestershire sauce
1 tablespoon prepared mustard
1 cup milk
½ cup bouillon
1 cup cubed cooked ham
4 strips pimiento

Split muffins, toast lightly. Melt butter or margarine in saucepan; stir flour smoothly in; add seasonings, Worcestershire, and mustard. Stir in milk and bouillon, and boil, stirring constantly until slightly thickened. Add ham. Place toasted muffins in bottom of greased small baking dish (one-quart). Pour creamed ham over them; crisscross pimiento strips on top. Set in very hot oven (475° F.) ten minutes until bubbly. 4 servings.

Mushrooms, green pepper, or sliced olives may be added with ham.

MENU

PINEAPPLE JUICE
CREAMED HAM ON ENGLISH MUFFINS
STRAWBERRY JAM FOR EXTRA MUFFINS
CANTALOUPE WITH SLICED BERRIES
COFFEE

HAMBURGER POTATO BAKE

1 pound ground beef
2 tablespoons minced peeled onion
Salt and pepper
4 medium-sized potatoes
2 tablespoons minced parsley
3 cups canned tomatoes, sieved
½ teaspoon Worcestershire sauce
½ teaspoon marjoram
¼ teaspoon basil

Mix meat with onion; season with one teaspoon salt and one-half teaspoon pepper. Spread in bottom of greased baking dish (two-quart). Scrub potatoes, rinse, drain, and pare. Slice very thin, in layers on top of meat. Season each layer with salt and pepper. Combine parsley, tomatoes, and Worcestershire. Pour over all. Cover dish. Bake in moderate oven (350° F.) twenty minutes. Uncover, and continue baking one-half hour. Sprinkle mixture with herbs; continue to bake thirty minutes, or until potatoes are done and browned. 4 to 6 servings.

Tastes good at brunch on a cold morning, or for supper.

MENU

HAMBURGER POTATO BAKE
PECAN COFFEE RING
SLICED PEACHES
COFFEE

(The Apple Kitchen)

CHICKEN APPLE SCALLOP

a delicious country-style casserole for a hearty luncheon

(PAGE 53)

(Mabel Stegner)

LAMB AND MUSHROOM PIE AU GRATIN

with toasted muffins, baked apples, and coffee, perfect for a simple meal

(PAGE 59)

PORK PIE WITH PASTRY TOP

a low-cost dinner delight, a favorite in any family

(PAGE 103)

(Mabel Stegner)

(Mabel Stegner)

SPAGHETTI AND LIVER CASSEROLE

as main dish for a supper party

(PAGE 154)

SPICED TURKISH TONGUES

for a candlelight supper with a foreign flavor

(PAGE 162)

(California Foods Research Institute)

MOCK CHICKEN CASSEROLE

a tasty way with leftover veal and sausage meat

(PAGE 200)

(California Foods Research Institute)

(Photo, Albert Gommi)

DANISH APPLE SAUCE DESSERT

garnished with candied cherries for easy, inexpensive eye-appeal

(PAGE 224)

(Photo, Albert Gommi)

MOCHA SOUFFLÉ

topped with cream or custard sauce, served with wine and coffee

(PAGE 241)

HAM AND HOMINY

2-pound slice smoked ham, cut in serving pieces
⅓ cup light cream
1 can (20-ounce) hominy
Freshly-ground pepper
2 small corn muffins, crumbled
2 tablespoons butter

Cook ham in skillet ten to fifteen minutes, or until done and lightly browned. Place in lightly-greased baking dish (one-quart). Add cream to drained hominy, mix and pour over ham. Season with pepper. Cover top with corn muffin crumbs; add dabs of butter. Bake in hot oven (450° F.) fifteen minutes, or until browned. 4 or 5 servings.

For Sausages and Hominy *substitute sausages for ham in this New England dish.*

MENU

STEWED PRUNES AND APRICOTS
HAM AND HOMINY
TOASTED BRIOCHE HONEY BUTTER
COFFEE

HOMINY AU GRATIN

1 can (20-ounce) hominy
¼ teaspoon salt
¼ teaspoon pepper
⅓ cup light cream
2 tablespoons butter or margarine
4 tablespoons buttered crumbs
2 tablespoons Parmesan cheese

Drain hominy; add salt, pepper, cream, and butter or margarine. Pour into buttered small, shallow au gratin dish. Cover top with crumbs and cheese. Bake in moderate oven (375° F.) twenty minutes, or until bubbly and browned. 4 servings.

Makes filling dish for a vegetable luncheon.

MENU

BAKED SHERRIED GRAPEFRUIT
HOMINY AU GRATIN
GRILLED SAUSAGES
MUFFINS AND CRANBERRY JELLY
COFFEE

GOLDEN MUSH WITH CHEESE

1½ cups yellow corn meal
4 cups boiling water
1½ teaspoons salt
2 cups grated mild Cheddar cheese
4 tablespoons butter, melted

Stir the corn meal into the rapidly boiling water. Add salt; reduce heat and let boil gently until very thick. Pour half of the mush into a buttered casserole (two-quart). Add half of the cheese and sprinkle with half of the melted butter. Repeat layers of mush, cheese, and butter. Bake in moderate oven (375° F.) thirty minutes, or until lightly browned. Serve warm. 6 to 8 servings.

Crisp bacon makes a fine-tasting garnish on this dish.

MENU

GRAPE JUICE
GOLDEN MUSH WITH CHEESE
CRISP BACON
PANETONE (ITALIAN FRUIT BREAD) ASSORTED JELLIES
COFFEE

HERBED SAUSAGE CAKES

1 pound sausage meat
1 cup canned tomato sauce
½ cup gravy or thin white sauce
½ teaspoon dry mustard
1 teaspoon prepared mustard
1 teaspoon brown sugar
1 teaspoon salt
½ teaspoon pepper
2 teaspoons mixed dried thyme, basil, marjoram, and fresh chives

Shape sausage meat into thin cakes. Cook in hot frying pan twenty minutes, or until well browned on all sides. Lift cakes with pancake turner into large lightly-greased shallow baking dish. Pour off half the fat. Stir tomato sauce, gravy or white sauce, and seasonings (not herbs) into frying pan. Mix, heat one or two minutes. Pour over sausage cakes in baking dish. Spoon herbs lightly over all. Bake in hot oven (450° F.) fifteen minutes, or until sauce is bubbly. 4 servings.

Small finger sausages are equally good prepared this way.

MENU

SLICED PEACHES AND CREAM
HERBED SAUSAGE CAKES
HOT CORN BREAD   QUINCE JELLY
COFFEE

WINTER BRUNCH SAUSAGE

1 pound sausage meat
2 cups canned kidney beans, or pork and beans in tomato sauce
Salt and pepper
2 tablespoons finely-chopped water cress
6 toast triangles

Cook sausage meat in shallow flameproof casserole (one and one-half quart) until browned and done. Drain off most of fat. Add beans; season with salt and pepper; add water cress. Cover; heat in hot oven (425° F.) twenty minutes; uncover, let cook five minutes more. Place toast triangles on top. Serve when bubbly. If beans have much liquid, drain off excess before adding to sausage. 6 servings.

Corn bread or blueberry muffins in order here.

MENU

STEWED PLUMS AND BLACK CHERRIES
WINTER BRUNCH SAUSAGE
BLUEBERRY MUFFINS
COFFEE

TOMATOES ON TOAST

2 large ripe tomatoes
Salt and pepper
Better Products curry seasoning, or any favorite curry powder
1 egg
1 tablespoon flour
¼ cup milk
4 slices bread
Butter
3 tablespoons Major Grey's chutney, chopped
1 tablespoon finely-chopped parsley
2 tablespoons bouillon or white wine

Wash tomatoes, peel, and cut in halves. Sprinkle cut surface with salt, pepper, and curry powder. Beat egg; mix with flour and milk. Cut bread in rounds, toast one side. Spread toasted side with butter then with drained chutney. Place rounds in shallow baking dish (one-quart). Dip seasoned tomato halves in batter, and place one half on each round of toast. Sprinkle tops with chopped parsley. Add bouillon or wine, mixed with the liquid from the chopped chutney, to the dish. Bake uncovered, in moderate oven (350° F.) twenty minutes, or until tomatoes are lightly browned and done. 4 servings.

Good for any meal, especially with roast fowl.

MENU

TOMATOES ON TOAST
PUFFY OMELET
BUTTERED RYE TOAST
STRAWBERRIES AND CREAM
COFFEE

TURKEY FOR BRUNCH

8 squares corn bread
8 large slices cooked turkey
8 slices crisply-cooked bacon
2 cups cheese sauce
4 tablespoons chopped toasted almonds

Place corn-bread squares in buttered shallow baking dish. Lay a slice of turkey on each square; place strip of bacon on turkey. Pour cheese sauce over each. Sprinkle with almonds. Place in hot oven (475° F.) until bubbly and browned. 8 servings.

Cheese Sauce: 1 cup medium white sauce; ½ teaspoon Worcestershire sauce; 1 cup grated American cheese. Heat together until cheese melts.

Make Chicken for Brunch, *and* Veal for Brunch *the same way.*

MENU

CRANBERRY JUICE
TURKEY FOR BRUNCH
EXTRA CORN BREAD
RAISIN-AND-NUT JAM
COFFEE

luncheon

in a covered dish

OVEN ARTICHOKES AND SHRIMP

1 can (20-ounce) artichoke hearts
2 tablespoons chopped peeled onion
2 tablespoons chopped parsley
1 tablespoon cut chives
1 teaspoon mixed basil, marjoram, dill
2 tablespoons French dressing
3 tablespoons grated mild cheese
1 package (14-ounce) quick-frozen shrimp, defrosted
¾ cup tomato juice
2 tablespoons lemon juice
1 teaspoon salt
Pepper and paprika
4 tablespoons butter
2 tablespoons sherry

Drain artichokes; arrange in border around shallow buttered baking dish (two-quart). Combine onion, parsley, chives, herbs, French dressing, and cheese, and sprinkle over artichokes. Heat cleaned shrimp with tomato and lemon juice; season with salt and pepper. Pour into center of baking dish. Add dabs of butter over artichokes and shrimp. Sprinkle shrimp lightly with sherry and paprika. Bake in moderate oven (350° F.) twenty-five minutes. 4 servings.

Or use another cooked vegetable in place of artichokes.

MENU

HONEYDEW MELON WITH SEEDLESS GRAPES
OVEN ARTICHOKES AND SHRIMP
CRESCENT CARAWAY ROLLS BLACK CURRANT JAM
TEA OR COFFEE

ASPARAGUS AU GRATIN

1½ pounds asparagus, or 2 packages quick-frozen, defrosted
1½ cups cheese sauce
4 very thin slices Cheddar cheese
Paprika

Wash asparagus; cut off woody ends; steam or boil vegetable until tips are tender, about twenty minutes. Drain. If quick-frozen asparagus is used, follow package directions for cooking. Arrange drained, cooked asparagus in a shallow baking dish. Cover with cheese sauce; then with sliced cheese. Sprinkle lightly with paprika. Bake in hot oven (475° F.) five minutes, or until cheese is melted and dish is bubbly. 6 servings.

Cheese Sauce: To 1 cup hot medium white sauce, add ½ cup grated Cheddar cheese, stir until cheese melts.

For Broccoli au Gratin *substitute broccoli for asparagus.*

MENU

MELON BALLS WITH SPRIG FRESH MINT
ASPARAGUS AU GRATIN
BROWN-AND-SERVE BISCUITS
ROLLED FRUIT PANCAKE
COFFEE

ASPARAGUS PARMESAN, NINO

1½ pounds asparagus, or 2 packages quick-frozen, defrosted
4 thin slices bread
6 tablespoons butter
1 tablespoon anchovy paste
¼ cup grated Parmesan cheese

Wash asparagus; cut off woody ends. Steam or boil vegetable until tips are tender, about twenty minutes. Drain. If quick-frozen asparagus is used, follow package directions for cooking. Trim bread, toast lightly on both sides. Mix three tablespoons butter with anchovy paste and spread toast. Arrange slices in shallow baking dish. Lay drained asparagus on toast. Melt remaining three tablespoons of butter and pour over asparagus; sprinkle with cheese. Place under broiler or in hot oven (475° F.) ten to fifteen minutes, until bubbly and cheese is browning. Serve at once. 4 servings.

Use your prettiest Limoges baker for this.

MENU

HOT TOMATO BOUILLON PAPRIKA CRACKERS
ASPARAGUS PARMESAN, NINO
BRANDIED BLACK CHERRIES SPONGECAKE
TEA OR COFFEE

BEEF TONGUE IN CHERRY SAUCE

8 slices boiled beef tongue
2 tablespoons red currant jelly
¼ cup port or claret
1 tablespoon Major Grey's chutney, chopped
1 teaspoon Worcestershire sauce
½ teaspoon A.1. or Harvey sauce
Juice 3 oranges
Juice 1 lemon
¼ teaspoon cayenne
2 tablespoons chopped candied cherries

Place sliced tongue in buttered Limoges or other shallow baking dish. Combine remaining ingredients except cherries. Mix well, and pour over tongue. Heat in moderate oven (350° F.) until bubbly and tongue is hot. Sprinkle cherries on top and serve. 4 servings.

Fit companion for a delicate spoon bread or soufflé.

MENU

HALF AVOCADO WITH LEMON FRENCH DRESSING
BEEF TONGUE IN CHERRY SAUCE
SPOON BREAD *
CREAM CHEESE GUAVA JELLY
WHOLE-WHEAT CRACKERS
COFFEE

BAKED CALAVO AND SHRIMP

1 pound raw shrimp
2 stalks celery
1 tablespoon lemon juice
¼ teaspoon cayenne
2 tablespoons each: butter, flour
½ cup each: milk, light cream
1 can (2-ounce) button mushrooms
Salt
2 Calavo avocados
3 tablespoons dry bread crumbs
8 anchovy fillets

Toss shrimp into six cups boiling water with celery, lemon juice, and cayenne. Simmer gently five minutes. Drain; rinse shrimp with cold water; remove shells; cut down the rounded back just under the surface and lift out sand vein with tip of knife. Melt butter and stir in flour. Gradually stir in milk and cream, and continue cooking until smooth and thick. Add drained mushrooms, shrimp, and one teaspoon salt. Cut Calavos in halves and remove seed and skin. Sprinkle halves with salt, and place in individual ramekins. Spoon shrimp mixture over avocados. Sprinkle with bread crumbs. Bake in moderately-low oven (300° F.) fifteen minutes. Top each serving with two anchovy fillets. 4 servings.

Favorite for California luncheons and patio suppers.

MENU

BAKED CALAVO AND SHRIMP
TOASTED CRACKERS
PINEAPPLE SHERBET COOKIES
COFFEE

CHEESE-AND-CABBAGE PUFF

4 slices bacon
4 tablespoons flour
4 tablespoons bacon fat
⅛ teaspoon pepper
1 cup milk
3 eggs
2 cups chopped cooked cabbage
½ cup grated Old English or Canadian white Cheddar cheese

Cook bacon crisp; drain, then crumble or cut in small pieces. Add flour to bacon fat, stir until smooth; add pepper and milk, stirring steadily over moderate heat. Continue to stir until thickened. Remove from heat. Beat egg yolks slightly; add sauce gradually to yolks; add drained cabbage, bacon, and cheese. Stir until well mixed. Whip egg whites stiff; fold into vegetable mixture. Pour into buttered baking dish (one and one-half quart). Set in shallow pan of hot water. Bake in moderate oven (325° F.) one hour. Serve at once. 5 or 6 servings.

For Cheese-and-Spinach Puff *substitute cooked spinach.*

MENU

SHRIMP AND GREEN PEPPER SALAD
CHEESE-AND-CABBAGE PUFF
SMALL BROWN-AND-SERVE WHOLE-WHEAT MUFFINS
PEAR BUTTER
BRANDIED COFFEE JELLY
COFFEE

CHEESE OLIVE SOUFFLÉ

¼ cup butter or margarine
¼ cup flour
¼ teaspoon salt
⅛ teaspoon pepper
¾ teaspoon dry mustard
½ teaspoon grated lemon peel
1 cup milk
1½ cups grated sharp Cheddar cheese
1 cup sliced ripe and green olives
1 cup soft bread crumbs
3 eggs

Melt butter or margarine in heavy saucepan over low heat. Add flour, salt, pepper, mustard, and lemon peel; stir until mixture is smooth. Remove from heat. Stir milk in gradually. Place over low heat and stir and cook ten minutes, until mixture is smooth and thick. Stir in cheese, olives, and crumbs. Remove from heat. Beat egg yolks until light. Stir slowly into hot mixture. Beat egg whites stiff. Gradually fold hot mixture into whites. Pour into an ungreased casserole (one and one-half quart). Set dish in shallow pan of hot water. Bake in moderately-low oven (300° F.) one hour and fifteen minutes. Serve at once. 6 servings.

Designed for luncheon, but popular at supper, too.

MENU

CHEESE OLIVE SOUFFLÉ
PICKLED CRAB APPLES   WATERMELON PICKLE
BUTTERED NUT BREAD   PISTACHIO ICE CREAM IN MERINGUE SHELL
TEA OR COFFEE

CHEESE—YOU NAME IT

4 slices day-old bread
1 cup cooked peas
1 jar (2½-ounce) dried beef
1 cup grated American cheese
½ cup chopped ripe olives
2 eggs
2 cups scalded milk
½ teaspoon salt
Black pepper

Cut bread into cubes. In greased baking dish (one and one-half quart) arrange layers of bread, peas, shredded beef, cheese, and olives. Beat eggs lightly; stir in milk, salt, and pepper. Pour over ingredients in casserole. Bake in moderate oven (325° F.) forty-five minutes or until set. 4 servings.

Fine flavor that satisfies any appetite.

MENU

CHEESE—YOU NAME IT
THIN FINGER CUCUMBER SANDWICHES
HONEYDEW MELON
COFFEE

TWO-CHEESE SOUFFLÉ

4 eggs
2 tablespoons butter or margarine, melted
1½ cups cottage cheese
2 tablespoons milk
3 tablespoons flour
¾ teaspoon salt
⅛ teaspoon white pepper
1 cup grated sharp Cheddar cheese

Beat egg yolks with butter or margarine until fluffy; use egg beater. Add cottage cheese, milk, flour, salt, and pepper; continue beating with egg beater until well blended. Beat egg whites stiff. Fold yolk mixture into whites with Cheddar cheese. Pour into unbuttered deep round baking dish (one and one-half quart; eight-inch diameter). Set in shallow pan of hot water. Bake in moderately-low oven (300° F.) one hour. Serve at once. 4 or 5 servings.

With one green vegetable, makes a delicious luncheon.

MENU

SHERRY ANCHOVY CANAPÉS
TWO-CHEESE SOUFFLÉ
ASPARAGUS VINAIGRETTE
APRICOT TART
COFFEE

CHICKEN IN PORT SAUCE

2 tablespoons butter or margarine
4 generous slices roast chicken
1 cup port
½ cup orange juice
1 tablespoon cognac
2 teaspoons lemon juice
½ tablespoon cornstarch
½ teaspoon salt
⅛ teaspoon freshly-ground pepper
⅛ teaspoon Tabasco sauce
1/16 teaspoon ground allspice
2 tablespoons pâté de foie gras

Melt butter or margarine in small flameproof casserole; heat chicken two minutes. Pour one-half cup port over and simmer two minutes. Push chicken to one side. Blend remaining ingredients together; stir into casserole, mix smoothly stirring until slightly thickened. Place chicken slices in sauce; cover dish and cook in hot oven (425° F.) ten minutes. 4 servings.

Prepare Duck in Port Sauce, *and* Turkey in Port Sauce *by the same recipe.*

MENU

ASSORTED MELON BALLS
CHICKEN IN PORT SAUCE
WILD RICE
SMALL POPPY-SEED ROLLS
PRUNE PIE
COFFEE

BAKED DEVILED CHICKEN

4-pound chicken, boiled or roasted
Prepared mustard (mild)
2 tablespoons chopped parsley
1 cup medium white sauce
1 teaspoon Worcestershire sauce
¼ cup heavy cream
Salt
Paprika

Slice chicken meat from bones. Arrange in buttered shallow baking dish (one-quart). Spread chicken generously with mustard. Sprinkle with parsley. Combine white sauce, Worcestershire, and cream. Add salt if needed. Pour over the chicken. Sprinkle lightly with paprika. Bake in moderate oven (350° F.) twenty-five minutes, until bubbly and browning. 6 servings.

Make Baked Deviled Beef, Veal, *or* Lamb *by the same recipe.*

MENU

MELON RING APPETIZER
(ROUND SLICE CANTALOUPE FILLED WITH ASSORTED MELON BALLS)
BAKED DEVILED CHICKEN GREEN BEANS
BUTTERED CRUSTY ITALIAN BREAD
COCONUT SNOWBALL OF CHOCOLATE CAKE
LEMON SHERBET
COFFEE

CHICKEN APPLE SCALLOP

(DEMETRIA TAYLOR, NEW YORK)

2 cups cubed cooked chicken
1 tablespoon prepared mustard
2 cups cooked sliced apples
1 tablespoon lemon juice
½ teaspoon salt
1 can (10½-ounce) condensed cream of mushroom soup
⅓ cup light cream
½ cup soft bread crumbs
2 tablespoons butter or margarine, melted

Combine chicken and mustard, and spread in a buttered baking dish (one-quart). Top with apple slices; sprinkle with lemon juice and salt. Combine soup and cream, and pour over all. Top with crumbs and butter or margarine. Bake in moderate oven (350° F.) twenty minutes, or until crumbs are brown. 4 servings.

For Tuna Apple Scallop *substitute tuna fish for chicken.*

MENU

HAM ROLL-UPS
(THIN SLICES BOILED HAM ROLLED AROUND SHARP CHEESE SPREAD)
CELERY HEARTS CARROT STICKS
CHICKEN APPLE SCALLOP
BROWN-AND-SERVE FRENCH BREAD
PORT WINE JELLY COLD CUSTARD SAUCE *
COFFEE

CHICKEN HOOSH-MI

(MARGARET AND NED CRANE, NEW YORK)

1 tablespoon chicken fat, butter, or margarine
4 each cooked carrots and small white onions
2 stalks celery
½ cup stuffing or bread crumbs
2 cups cubed cooked chicken
1 cup gravy or thick poultry stock
Onion salt, poultry seasoning, herbs, Parmesan cheese
1 egg yolk
2 tablespoons sherry or dry white wine
2 tablespoons cooked peas

Heat fat in flameproof casserole (one and one-half quart). Slice vegetables in bite-sized pieces into the fat; brown lightly. Add stuffing or crumbs, chicken, and gravy or stock; mix well. Season with onion salt, poultry seasoning, and herbs to taste depending on amount of seasoning already in stuffing and gravy. Sprinkle mixture lightly with Parmesan cheese. Bake, uncovered, in moderately-hot oven (400° F.) ten minutes. In small saucepan beat egg yolk until light. Very slowly add about three-fourths cup of the hot liquid from the casserole to the yolk stirring smoothly; add to casserole stirring well through the mixture. Add wine and peas. Mix. Bake about five minutes longer. 4 servings.

"Hoosh-Mi" from Marion Crawford's "The Little Princesses."

MENU

TOMATO JUICE SESAME-SEED CRACKERS
CHICKEN HOOSH-MI HOT RICE
SMALL MUFFINS
HONEYDEW MELON FRESH LIME
MADEIRA OR PORT
COFFEE

BALTIMORE DEVILED CRAB MEAT

1 pound (2 cups) cooked, canned, or quick-frozen crab meat
5 tablespoons butter or margarine
1 tablespoon flour
½ teaspoon salt
¾ teaspoon dry mustard
½ teaspoon paprika
⅛ teaspoon nutmeg
1 cup light cream
3 tablespoons minced parsley
2 tablespoons lemon juice
12 large potato chips

Remove all cartilage from crab meat, and flake it. Melt four tablespoons of butter or margarine; stir in flour, salt, mustard, paprika, and nutmeg. Add cream slowly, stirring constantly over low heat until mixture thickens and boils. Stir in parsley, lemon juice, and crab meat. Pour into greased shallow baking dish (one-quart). Crumble potato chips over the top. Add dabs of the remaining tablespoon of butter. Bake in moderate oven (375° F.) ten minutes, or until top is browning. 6 servings.

Or use individual scallop shells; garnish with parsley.

MENU

BALTIMORE DEVILED CRAB MEAT
TOSSED MIXED GREEN SALAD CORN-BREAD STICKS
CHOCOLATE CHIFFON PIE COFFEE

SLICED DUCK IN ORANGE SAUCE

8 slices leftover roast duck
2 oranges
Juice 1 lemon
½ teaspoon Worcestershire sauce
½ cup bouillon
1 cup leftover gravy
Salt
Cayenne

Place sliced roast duck in greased Limoges, or other shallow baker. Cut the thin outer peel of one orange in strips; pour boiling water over it, and boil five minutes; drain. Combine strips with juice of both oranges, lemon juice, Worcestershire, bouillon, and gravy. Add salt if needed, and a dash of cayenne. Heat until steaming. Pour over meat. Place in moderate oven (375° F.) until bubbly. Serve hot. 4 servings.

For Sliced Ham in Orange Sauce *substitute baked ham.*

MENU

BEET AND WATER-CRESS SALAD
SLICED DUCK IN ORANGE SAUCE
POTATOES AU GRATIN
BOSTON BROWN BREAD
BEL PAESE CHEESE FRESH PEARS
COFFEE

CURRIED EGGS AND CHEESE

4 slices rusk or bread, buttered
¾ cup grated Cheddar cheese
1½ teaspoons Better Products curry seasoning, or curry powder
4 eggs
½ teaspoon salt
¼ teaspoon pepper
¼ teaspoon paprika
1 cup milk

Arrange rusk or bread in buttered baking dish. Cover thickly with cheese; sprinkle curry powder over cheese. Beat eggs; combine with seasonings, and milk. Pour over the cheese. Bake in moderate oven (350° F.) twenty-five minutes, or until lightly risen and browned. Serve at once. 4 servings.

Garnish of green pepper rings adds another good flavor.

MENU

TOMATO ASPIC APPETIZER
(CUBED AND SERVED ON LETTUCE WITH CHIVE MAYONNAISE)
CURRIED EGGS AND CHEESE
EXTRA TOAST
DUTCH APPLE CAKE CREAM
COFFEE

SPICY HAM AND EGGS

¾ cup ripe olives
3 tablespoons butter or margarine
3 tablespoons flour
1 teaspoon dry mustard
¾ teaspoon salt
⅛ teaspoon black pepper
1½ cups milk
1 teaspoon prepared horse-radish
1 teaspoon Worcestershire sauce
1 tablespoon chili sauce
⅛ teaspoon Tabasco sauce
2 cups diced cooked ham
4 hard-cooked eggs, sliced
¾ cup diced American cheese

Cut olives in large pieces. Melt butter or margarine in a saucepan; blend in flour, mustard, salt, and pepper. Add milk, horse-radish, Worcestershire, chili sauce, and Tabasco. Arrange alternate layers of ham, sliced eggs, olives, sauce, and cheese in buttered shallow baking dish (one and one-half quart). Bake in moderately-hot oven (400° F.) twenty-five to thirty minutes. 4 or 5 servings.

Spicy Turkey and Eggs, Spicy Chicken and Eggs, *made by same recipe.*

MENU

SPICY HAM AND EGGS
OVEN-TOASTED ITALIAN BREAD
(CUT THIN, SPREAD WITH OLIVE OIL, BROWNED IN HOT OVEN)
DEEP-DISH PEACH PIE
COFFEE

LAMB AND MUSHROOM PIE AU GRATIN

¼ cup butter or margarine
2 tablespoons chopped peeled onion
¼ cup flour
1 teaspoon salt
⅛ teaspoon each: pepper, nutmeg, rosemary
1 can (6-ounce) broiled mushrooms
1½ cups milk
2 cups chopped cooked lamb
2½ cups cooked carrots-and-peas
½ cup grated Cheddar cheese

Melt butter or margarine in saucepan over moderate heat. Add onion and cook about one minute. Stir in flour, salt, pepper, nutmeg, and rosemary. Drain mushrooms; save broth. Combine mushroom broth and milk; stir into flour mixture. Cook, stirring constantly, until sauce thickens and boils. Reserve twelve mushrooms for garnish; chop remainder coarsely and add to sauce. Add lamb and all but one-half cup of the cooked vegetables. Mix lightly and pour into four greased shallow individual baking dishes. Sprinkle tops of casseroles with cheese. Bake in moderate oven (375° F.) about twenty minutes until bubbly and cheese is lightly browned. Five minutes before ready to serve, garnish tops of casseroles with reserved mushrooms and the one-half cup vegetables. 4 servings.

For Beef and Mushroom Pie au Gratin *use cooked beef.*

MENU

LAMB AND MUSHROOM PIE AU GRATIN
TOASTED AND BUTTERED ENGLISH MUFFINS BAKED APPLES
COFFEE

LEEKS AU GRATIN

1 bunch (16) leeks
4 tablespoons butter or margarine, melted
½ teaspoon salt
¼ cup consommé or bouillon
1 egg yolk
2 tablespoons grated Parmesan cheese

Wash leeks; drain; remove root ends and green tops, leaving about two inches above the white portion. Cook covered in a large amount of boiling salted water twenty to thirty minutes, until just tender. Drain. Place in shallow baking dish (one-quart). Mix butter or margarine, salt, consommé or bouillon, and beaten egg yolk. Pour over leeks; sprinkle with cheese. Brown in a moderately-hot oven (400° F.) ten to fifteen minutes. 4 servings.

For a luncheon main dish, line baking dish with toast points.

MENU

SLICED TOMATOES AND ANCHOVY-STUFFED EGGS
(HARD-COOKED EGGS, HALVED AND STUFFED)
LEEKS AU GRATIN
SLICED COLD TURKEY
DEEP-DISH PLUM PIE
TEA OR COFFEE

ITALIAN BAKED MUSHROOMS

1½ pounds mushrooms
3 tablespoons chopped parsley
1 sliver garlic, chopped
1 teaspoon orégano
¾ cup coarse bread crumbs
¼ cup grated Parmesan cheese
1 teaspoon salt
½ teaspoon pepper
¼ cup olive oil
¼ cup bouillon or hot water

Wash mushrooms; peel caps; slice into oiled baking dish (one and one-half quart). Sprinkle with parsley, garlic, orégano, half of the crumbs, and half of the cheese. Season with half of the salt and pepper. Pour the oil over all. Add remaining crumbs, cheese, and seasonings. Bake in moderate oven (350° F.) twenty-five minutes, or until mushrooms are tender and top browned. If dish seems dry after fifteen minutes baking, add a little bouillon or hot water. Serve hot. 6 servings.

To vary, add one cup creamed chicken before last crumbs.

MENU

PROSCIUTTO AND HONEYDEW MELON
ITALIAN BAKED MUSHROOMS
CHIANTI
BUTTERED ZUCCHINI CRUSTY ITALIAN BREAD
MOCHA REFRIGERATOR CAKE COFFEE

MUSHROOM-VEGETABLE PIE

3 tablespoons fat
1 cup chopped peeled onions
3 tablespoons flour
1 cup well-seasoned chicken broth
1 can (3-ounce) chopped broiled mushrooms
1 cup each: chopped cooked celery, carrots
1 cup cooked peas
½ teaspoon salt
⅛ teaspoon pepper
⅛ teaspoon rosemary
½ teaspoon Kitchen Bouquet
1 cup biscuit-mix

Melt fat in saucepan over moderate heat. Add onions, and cook about ten minutes until barely tender, stirring frequently. Stir in flour. Add chicken broth and cook, stirring constantly, until sauce thickens. Add contents of can of mushrooms, celery, carrots, peas, seasonings, and Kitchen Bouquet. Bring to boiling; lower heat and simmer five minutes. Prepare biscuit-mix according to directions on package. Roll into circle about seven inches in diameter. Cut in six wedge-shaped pieces. Pour vegetables into greased shallow eight-inch baking dish. Arrange biscuit topping. Bake in hot oven (425° F.) fifteen minutes or until biscuit is done and browned. Serve immediately. 4 to 6 servings.

Just as good when baked in individual dishes.

MENU

CONSOMMÉ WITH POPPY-SEED CRACKERS
MUSHROOM-VEGETABLE PIE
CHOCOLATE PUDDING LEMON COOKIES COFFEE

NOODLES ROMANOFF

(HELEN AND CHARLES HOVEY, NEW YORK)

⅔ cup noodles
1 cup cottage cheese
1 cup sour cream
¼ cup chopped peeled onions
½ clove garlic, peeled and chopped fine
2 teaspoons Worcestershire sauce
⅛ teaspoon Tabasco sauce
½ teaspoon salt
½ cup grated Cheddar cheese

Cook noodles as described on the package. Drain. Add cottage cheese, sour cream, onions, garlic, sauces, and salt. Combine well. Place in an eight-inch buttered casserole. Bake in a moderate oven (350° F.) thirty minutes. Remove from oven, sprinkle grated cheese liberally over top, and return to the oven for ten minutes. 6 servings.

Garlic may be omitted for a ladies' luncheon.

MENU

FRESH FRUIT CUP
(APPLE SLICES, BLACK GRAPES, FRESH PINEAPPLE, ORANGE CUBES)
NOODLES ROMANOFF
SMALL WHOLE-WHEAT ROLLS
ALMONDS COINTREAU
COFFEE

LUNCHEON POTATO PUFF

3 cups hot mashed potatoes (5 or 6 medium-sized potatoes)
4 tablespoons butter or margarine, melted
1 cup bread crumbs
⅓ cup mayonnaise
1 teaspoon salt
½ teaspoon basil
1 tablespoon grated lemon peel
1½ tablespoons lemon juice
½ cup milk
3 eggs
¼ cup grated Cheddar cheese

Prepare mashed potatoes. Combine melted butter or margarine with crumbs, and spread in shallow nine-inch casserole. Combine mayonnaise, salt, basil, lemon peel, and juice, milk, and beaten egg yolks. Add to mashed potatoes and beat until smooth and fluffy. Beat egg whites stiff; fold into potato mixture. Pour into crumbed casserole. Sprinkle cheese over top. Bake in moderate oven (350° F.) thirty minutes. Turn oven to 375° F. and bake ten minutes, or until browned. 6 servings.

Add chopped leftover ham or beef tongue for variation.

MENU

LUNCHEON POTATO PUFF
SPICY LEMON GELATIN SALAD ON MIXED GREENS
FRENCH DRESSING
SWEDISH RYE BREAD
RED RASPBERRIES CREAM
COFFEE

MASHED POTATOES WITH DRIED BEEF

4 or 5 potatoes, boiled
Salt and pepper
3 cups milk
¼ pound sliced dried beef
4 tablespoons butter or margarine
3 tablespoons flour
¼ teaspoon pepper
½ cup coarse crumbs

Mash potatoes, season; add one cup hot milk slowly, whipping potatoes until light. Use only enough hot milk to make fluffy, light potatoes. Tear dried beef in small pieces. Melt three tablespoons butter or margarine in suaçepan, add beef, and sauté five minutes, or until light brown. Sprinkle with flour and pepper, and mix well. Add remaining two cups of milk slowly, stirring constantly over low heat until mixture thickens and boils. Let cook until well thickened. Pour creamed beef into a greased baking dish (one and one-half quart). Pile mashed potatoes on top. Scatter crumbs thickly over potatoes; add remaining butter or margarine in dabs. Bake in moderate oven (350° F.) thirty minutes, or until browned. 6 servings.

Use creamed leftover lamb or chicken in the same recipe.

MENU

ARTICHOKE HEARTS IN FRENCH DRESSING
RIPE OLIVES
MASHED POTATOES WITH DRIED BEEF
BUTTERED PUMPERNICKEL GRAPE JAM
LEMON MERINGUE TART COFFEE

BAKED SHRIMP CREOLE

2 cups cooked, canned, or quick-frozen shrimp
4 tablespoons butter or margarine
½ teaspoon paprika
2 stalks celery, chopped
2 small onions, peeled and chopped
1 green pepper, chopped
1 can (20-ounce) tomatoes
½ clove garlic, peeled and chopped
½ bay leaf
¼ teaspoon thyme
2 tablespoons chopped parsley
1 teaspoon salt
¼ teaspoon chili powder

If quick-frozen shrimp are used, defrost according to directions on package. Remove black line from shrimp; wash and drain. Heat two tablespoons butter or margarine in shallow flameproof baking dish (two-quart); sprinkle shrimp lightly with paprika; sauté two minutes. Push shrimp to one side; add remaining butter or margarine, celery, onions, and green pepper. Cook about six minutes, until vegetables are lightly browned. Mix with shrimp; add tomatoes, garlic, herbs, and seasoning. Cover dish. Bake in hot oven (475° F.) twenty minutes. Serve with hot rice. 4 servings.

A *Southern favorite, winter and summer.*

MENU

BROILED SHERRIED GRAPEFRUIT
BAKED SHRIMP CREOLE RICE
PINEAPPLE SHERBET POUNDCAKE
COFFEE

HATFIELD DEVILED SHRIMP

(MARGARET AND NED CRANE, NEW YORK)

1 tablespoon butter or margarine
1 small onion, peeled and chopped fine
1 tablespoon chopped olives
2 tablespoons tomato sauce
1 teaspoon English or French mustard
1 cup poultry-stuffing crumbs (or leftover dressing)
1 cup thick stock, gravy, or white sauce
1 egg yolk
1 tablespoon heavy cream
2 cups cooked, canned, or quick-frozen cleaned shrimp
½ cup cooked peas

Heat butter or margarine in flameproof casserole (one and one-half quart). Add onion and brown lightly. Add olives, tomato sauce, and mustard; stir and mix. Add crumbs or dressing. Mix and cook two minutes. Add stock, gravy, or white sauce. Mix well; let simmer three minutes. Beat egg yolk until fluffy; add cream; slowly add two tablespoons of sauce from the casserole. Add shrimp to casserole; add egg-and-cream mixture, and peas. Mix well. Bake in hot oven (425° F.) ten minutes, or until bubbly. Serve with rice. 4 servings.

A fine way to use up leftover dressing and gravy.

MENU

HATFIELD DEVILED SHRIMP
FRENCH BREAD SPREAD WITH HERB BUTTER
TINY CREAM PUFFS WITH HOT CHOCOLATE SAUCE
COFFEE

PALERMO BAKED SHRIMP

1½ pounds fresh jumbo shrimp
1 tablespoon Better Products curry seasoning, or curry powder
2 tablespoons olive oil
1 teaspoon salt
½ teaspoon pepper
¼ teaspoon saffron
½ cup bouillon
1 cup dry white wine

Shell shrimp; clean, wash, and drain. Heat curry powder three minutes in shallow flameproof metal-base, baking dish (one and one-half quart). Stir oil in, and mix. Sauté shrimp six minutes. Add salt and pepper. Stir saffron into bouillon, mix; pour over shrimp; add wine to dish. Cover and bake in moderately-hot oven (400° F.) fifteen minutes; uncover and bake five minutes. Liquid should be cooked down around shrimp. Serve on hot rice. 6 servings.

Some Italian cooks add one or two slices finocchio to this dish.

MENU

PALERMO BAKED SHRIMP
RICE
FRESH FRUIT SALAD
(SLICED PEACHES, PLUMS, COTTAGE CHEESE)
ORANGE FRENCH DRESSING
GINGER COOKIES
TEA OR COFFEE

SCALLOPED TOMATOES AU GRATIN

1 can (1-pound) tomatoes
1 small onion, peeled and chopped
1 tablespoon sugar
½ teaspoon salt
½ teaspoon pepper
¼ teaspoon celery salt
¼ teaspoon basil
4 slices toast
2 tablespoons butter or margarine, melted
¼ cup grated Cheddar cheese

Combine tomatoes with onion, sugar, seasonings, and basil. Cut two slices of toast in cubes. Cut crusts from remaining slices, and cut slices in triangles for top of dish. Pour layer of tomatoes into buttered shallow baking dish (one-quart). Cover with toast cubes; add remaining tomatoes. Cover with toast triangles. Pour butter or margarine on toast; sprinkle cheese over all. Bake in moderate oven (375° F.) twenty minutes, or until dish is bubbly and cheese browned. 4 or 5 servings.

An old favorite for simple meals, summer and winter.

MENU

CRANBERRY JUICE CELERY CRACKERS
OVEN-BROILED CHICKEN BREASTS
SCALLOPED TOMATOES AU GRATIN
SMALL ORANGE BISCUITS
RAISIN-AND-NUT JAM
COFFEE

TUNA-AND-MUSHROOM RING

1 can (7-ounce) tuna fish
2½ cups bread crumbs
½ cup milk, scalded
1½ cups chopped canned mushrooms
2 tablespoons butter or margarine
2 eggs
1¼ cups thick white sauce
1 tablespoon chopped pimiento
1 tablespoon chopped parsley
1 tablespoon grated peeled onion
½ teaspoon salt
¼ teaspoon pepper

Drain fish; flake and put through food chopper using fine knife. Soften crumbs in milk. Sauté mushrooms in butter or margarine three minutes. Beat eggs and combine with white sauce. Add all ingredients and mix well. Place in greased ring pan (one and one-half quart). Set ring in shallow pan of hot water. Bake in moderate oven (350° F.) fifty to sixty minutes. Turn out onto warmed platter. Fill center with creamed mixed vegetables. 6 servings.

Also good cold, sliced, and served with a hot cream sauce.

MENU

TUNA-AND-MUSHROOM RING WITH CREAMED PEAS
TOASTED CHEESE BREAD BLACK CURRANT JAM
BAKED PLUMS SMALL LEMON CUPCAKES
TEA OR COFFEE

COUNTRY CLUB TURKEY

1½ pounds asparagus spears, cooked
½ cup ripe olives
1 can (10½-ouncc) crcam of chickcn soup
½ teaspoon grated peeled onion
⅛ teaspoon nutmeg
½ cup diced pimiento
1 cup cubed cooked turkey
2 tablespoons grated smoked cheese

Drain asparagus. Place in greased shallow baking dish or pie plate. Cut olives from pits in large pieces. Mix with soup, onion, nutmeg, pimiento, and turkey. Pour over asparagus. Top with cheese. Bake in moderate oven (350° F.) twenty-five to thirty minutes. 3 to 4 servings.

Try this for luncheon after the Christmas turkey dinner.

MENU

GRAPEFRUIT JUICE POPPY-SEED CRACKERS
COUNTRY CLUB TURKEY
THIN WATER-CRESS SANDWICHES
LEMON SHERBET COCONUT MACAROONS
TEA COFFEE

dinners,
easy and delicious

SHORT RIBS WITH HERBS

6 short ribs of beef (½ pound each)
3 tablespoons beef suet or shortening
1 clove garlic, peeled and chopped
3 leeks, sliced thin
1 can (8-ounce) tomato sauce
1 teaspoon salt
¼ teaspoon each: pepper, chili powder, rosemary, basil

Wipe meat with wet cloth. Brown ribs in suet or shortening in large skillet. Push meat to one side and sauté garlic and leeks five minutes. Mix tomato sauce and seasonings (not herbs) and stir into garlic and leeks. Heat two minutes. Place browned ribs in casserole. Spoon sauce over and around meat. Cover casserole. Bake in moderate oven (325° F.) one and one-half hours. Add herbs to dish, cover and bake half an hour longer. Skim off excess fat. 6 servings.

A favorite dish for a hungry family.

MENU

RADISHES STUFFED CELERY
SHORT RIBS WITH HERBS
WILD RICE
ARTICHOKE HEARTS ON LETTUCE FRENCH DRESSING
POPPY-SEED ROLLS
APRICOT SHERBET
COFFEE

CASSEROLE BEEF STEW

2 pounds boneless beef shank or chuck, cut in 1-inch cubes
1 tablespoon shortening
1 clove garlic, peeled and chopped
1 can (8-ounce) tomato sauce
1 cup water or bouillon
1 teaspoon salt
1 teaspoon sugar
½ teaspoon celery salt
¼ teaspoon dry mustard
¼ teaspoon pepper
12 small white onions, peeled
2 tablespoons chopped parsley

Trim any fat from beef; brown meat well in fat trimmings and shortening in (metal-base) flameproof casserole. Add garlic, tomato sauce, water or bouillon, and seasonings. Stir; cook ten minutes. Cover and place in moderate oven (325° F.). Cook one hour. Add onions; cover and continue cooking thirty minutes, or until onions are tender. Sprinkle top with minced parsley and serve. 6 servings.

A bottle of favorite red wine turns it into a glamour dish.

MENU

GREEN TURTLE SOUP CHEESE STICKS
CASSEROLE BEEF STEW
BROWN-AND-SERVE FRENCH BREAD
HONEYDEW MELON
COINTREAU COFFEE

CASSEROLE OF BEEF

(FLORENCE AND PETER GREIG, NEW YORK)

1 tablespoon French olive oil
2 cups 1-inch cubes cooked beef
1 can (10½-ounce) Campbell's condensed oxtail soup
1 cup red wine
2 Herbox bouillon cubes
½ cup cubed carrots
8 small white onions, peeled
½ cup peas or small Lima beans
1 cup potato balls

Heat oil in (metal-base) flameproof casserole. Brown meat on all sides. Add soup. Heat wine in small saucepan, and dissolve bouillon cubes in it; add to casserole, stirring well. Add vegetables. Cover, and cook in moderate oven (350° F.) one and one-half to two hours, or until potatoes are cooked. If more liquid is needed during cooking, add mixture of wine and bouillon, stir into casserole. 4 servings.

A delicious use for leftover roast.

MENU

JELLIED MADRILÈNE
CASSEROLE OF BEEF CRISP SALT-RYE ROLLS
RED WINE
LETTUCE WITH ROQUEFORT CHEESE DRESSING
STRAWBERRIES COFFEE

SAVORY BRAISED STEAK

2 pounds chuck steak
¼ cup flour
1½ teaspoon salt
¼ teaspoon pepper
½ teaspoon paprika
1 large onion, peeled and sliced
3 tablespoons shortening or beef suet
½ cup boiling water
½ cup tomato juice
½ bay leaf
½ teaspoon orégano
½ cup port or claret

Dredge steak with flour mixed with the salt, pepper, and paprika. Pound well. Cook onion in shortening or suet in (metal-base) flameproof baking dish five minutes; add steak, and brown lightly on both sides. Add water, tomato juice, and bay leaf. Cover; bake in moderate oven (350° F.) one hour. Baste several times during the hour, adding more hot water and tomato juice if needed. Add orégano and wine, and let bake fifteen minutes more. 4 or 5 servings.

Succulent and delicious. Middle Western dinner favorite.

MENU

COCKTAILS SARDINE CANAPÉS
SAVORY BRAISED STEAK
PAPRIKA RICE BUTTERED ASPARAGUS
BROWN-AND-SERVE ROLLS
PEARS IN RED WINE * COFFEE

STEAK BAKED IN SOUR CREAM

1½ pounds round steak cut 1-inch thick
Salt and pepper
2 tablespoons fat
1 cup canned tomatoes, sieved
½ teaspoon A.1. sauce
½ teaspoon dry mustard
¾ cup sour cream

Wipe meat with a wet cloth. Season steak on both sides with salt and pepper. Brown in fat, in a (metal-base) flameproof baking dish. Mix tomatoes with seasonings and pour over meat. Cover and bake in moderate oven (375° F.) until the steak is tender, about thirty minutes. Add the sour cream, and cook uncovered ten minutes more. (If sour cream is too thick, mix with a little light cream.) 4 servings.

Chopped button mushrooms make a good addition to this steak.

MENU

COLESLAW APPETIZER
STEAK BAKED IN SOUR CREAM
BAKED POTATOES
CHEESE BREAD
CHERRY-APPLE COMPOTE *
COFFEE

CHICKEN MARSALA

Small roasting chicken, quartered
4 tablespoons butter or margarine
1 pint Marsala
½ clove garlic, peeled and chopped
1 teaspoon dried herbs: majoram, basil, rosemary
3 whole cloves
1½ teaspoons salt
½ teaspoon pepper
½ teaspoon paprika
4 tablespoons grated Gruyère cheese

Brown chicken in butter or margarine, in flameproof (metal base) baking dish. Add Marsala, garlic, herbs, cloves, salt, and pepper. Cover; bake in moderate oven (325° F.) one hour. Baste frequently during baking with liquid in the dish. Uncover dish, and let bake and brown thirty minutes. Sprinkle top with paprika and generously with cheese; continue to bake twenty minutes, or until cheese is melted and browning. 4 servings.

Conversation piece: double recipe, cook in two casseroles for buffet party.

MENU

COCKTAILS COCKTAIL SAUSAGES CRISP CRACKERS
CHICKEN MARSALA
GREEN BEAN AND SPANISH ONION SALAD FRENCH DRESSING
TINY SWEET ROLLS
PEACHES WITH CURAÇAO
COFFEE

CHICKEN PAPRIKA

1 large, plump frying chicken cut in serving pieces
½ tablespoon salt
4 tablespoons butter or margarine
2 small onions, peeled and chopped
2 teaspoons paprika
1 tablespoon flour
2 cups bouillon or consommé
1 tablespoon heavy cream
1 cup sour cream
2 tablespoons chopped fresh dill

Season chicken with salt. Heat butter or margarine in heavy (metal-base) flameproof baking dish (two-quart) until light brown; add onions, and cook six minutes; add paprika, and mix well. Brown chicken fifteen minutes, or until golden. Cover, and bake in moderate oven (350° F.) thirty minutes, or until chicken is done. Sprinkle with flour. Add bouillon or consommé and heavy cream; stir sauce to mix well, spooning it over the chicken. Cover and bake fifteen minutes longer. Push chicken to one end of casserole; stir sour cream into sauce, mix and boil three minutes. Spoon well over chicken. Sprinkle top with dill and serve. 6 servings.

Hungarian favorite; some cooks omit the dill.

MENU

CHICKEN PAPRIKA BUTTERED NOODLES
RHINE WINE
ROMAINE AND ORANGE SALAD ORANGE FRENCH DRESSING
BAKED CHOCOLATE PUDDING * COFFEE

COQ AU VIN

Large frying chicken, cut in serving pieces
Salt and pepper
½ cup diced fat salt pork
2 tablespoons butter or margarine
6 small onions, peeled
2 cans (6-ounce) broiled mushrooms
3 shallots, chopped
1 clove garlic, peeled and chopped
2 tablespoons flour
2 cups claret or Burgundy
Bouillon, if required
Herb bouquet (3 sprigs parsley, small stalk celery, ½ bay leaf, sprig thyme, tied together with thread)
2 tablespoons chopped parsley

Season chicken with salt and pepper. Cook salt pork with butter or margarine in flameproof deep metal casserole until golden; remove pork and save it. Sauté chicken in fat twenty minutes, or until golden brown on all sides. Add onions and mushrooms, cover dish, and continue cooking over low heat twenty minutes, or until onions are soft and beginning to brown. Pour off half the fat. Add shallots and garlic to casserole; sprinkle with flour, stir and let cook five minutes. Add wine and stir well. If necessary, add a little bouillon. There should be enough liquid to just cover chicken. Add herb bouquet and cooked pork. Cover casserole. Place in moderately-hot oven (400° F.) and cook forty-five minutes, or until chicken is done. Remove herb bouquet. Sprinkle top of casserole with chopped parsley before serving. 4 to 6 servings.

Some cooks prefer less garlic, and more herbs.

MENU

COCKTAILS PÂTÉ DE FOIE GRAS THIN BUTTERED TOAST
COQ AU VIN
POTATO BALLS, PAPRIKA BUTTER FRENCH ROLLS
MACEDOINE OF FRUIT
(SEEDLESS GRAPES, APRICOTS, ORANGE WITH KIRSCH)
LARGE SOFT MACAROONS COFFEE

EASY CHICKEN FRICASSEE

4-pound chicken, cut in serving pieces
½ cup flour
1 teaspoon salt
¼ teaspoon pepper
¼ teaspoon paprika
4 tablespoons butter or margarine
1 can (10½-ounce) mushroom soup
1 soup can milk
1 can (6-ounce) broiled mushrooms
½ bay leaf
1 medium-sized onion, peeled and sliced
Light cream or top milk, as required

Place chicken pieces in paper bag with flour, salt, pepper, and paprika. Close tightly, and shake to coat all pieces evenly. Brown well on all sides in hot fat, in shallow flameproof (metal-base) baking dish, about twenty-five minutes. Spoon any excess fat up over chicken. Mix soup with milk; add with mushrooms, bay leaf, and onion to baking dish. Cover; bake in moderately-low oven (300° F.) one hour, or until chicken is done. Add a little light cream, or top milk, to dish if sauce cooks down too much. 6 servings.

Old favorite, always welcomed by hungry family and guests.

MENU

VEGETABLE JUICE COCKTAIL POTATO CHIPS
EASY CHICKEN FRICASSEE
BROILED TOMATOES
ENDIVE SALAD FRENCH DRESSING
BROWN BREAD
BLACK RASPBERRY SHERBET COFFEE

GOOBER CHICKEN CASSEROLE

2 chicken breasts, halved, or
  1 small frying chicken, cut in serving pieces
Better Products chicken seasoning
4 tablespoons butter or margarine
½ cup bouillon
1 cup chopped peanuts
1 cup cream
½ cup sour cream

Sprinkle chicken with a tablespoon special seasoning. (If Better Products seasoning is not available, use a mixture of salt, pepper, paprika, and celery salt.) Brown chicken in butter or margarine, in flameproof (metal-base) casserole. Pour bouillon around chicken; place casserole in moderate oven (350° F.) and bake forty-five minutes. Mix peanuts, cream, and sour cream, and pour over chicken. Add another light sprinkling of seasoning, and continue baking fifteen minutes. (Double recipe for buffet supper.) 4 servings.

A conversation dinner speciality from Mississippi.

MENU

CLAM-AND-TOMATO JUICE COCKTAIL
GOOBER CHICKEN CASSEROLE
GREEN BEANS WITH MUSHROOMS
CRUSTY FRENCH BREAD WITH HERB BUTTER
MANY-LAYER FRENCH CHOCOLATE CAKE (BAKERY)
COFFEE

HERBED OVEN CHICKEN

3 plump chicken breasts, halved
5 tablespoons olive oil
Juice 2 lemons
½ teaspoon each: dried thyme, basil, marjoram
1 tablespoon cut fresh chives
Flour, salt, pepper
1 tablespoon minced parsley
Paprika

Wipe chicken breasts with wet cloth. Dry; place in bowl. Pour three tablespoons oil over chicken; squeeze juice of one lemon over, and sprinkle with mixed herbs and chives. Cover dish, and let stand in refrigerator three or four hours. Drain chicken, saving marinade; sprinkle lightly with flour, and brown twenty minutes in two tablespoons hot oil. Use large shallow flameproof (metal-base) baking dish so chicken makes only one layer. Sprinkle lightly with salt and pepper. Mix marinade with about one cup hot water, the parsley, and juice of remaining lemon. Pour into baking dish. Sprinkle chicken with paprika. Cover and bake in moderate oven (375° F.) about thirty minutes. Uncover and bake until chicken is done. Baste frequently with sauce in dish. 6 servings.

Make Herbed Oven Turkey *using small frying turkey; bake two hours.*

MENU

FRESH FRUIT CUP
(CHERRIES, STRAWBERRIES, ORANGE)
HERBED OVEN CHICKEN POTATOES AU GRATIN
BUTTERED PEAS
WHOLE-WHEAT ROLLS PINEAPPLE MARMALADE
CARAMEL CUSTARD COFFEE

PARMESAN CHICKEN RING

1⅓ cups Minute rice
⅛ teaspoon salt
½ cup boiling chicken consommé
1 cup boiling water
3 tablespoons grated Parmesan cheese
2 tablespoons butter or margarine
½ teaspoon celery salt
2 eggs, slightly beaten with
1 cup milk
1 cup cubed cooked chicken

Add rice and salt to rapidly-boiling consommé and water in a saucepan; mix with a fork, just enough to moisten rice. Cover and remove from heat. Let stand thirteen minutes. (If regular rice is used boil it in three cups consommé thinned with two cups water, until tender; do not stir; drain.)

Using fork, lightly mix cheese, butter or margarine, and celery salt into hot rice. Add eggs, milk, and chicken. Pour into buttered ring mold (one and one-half quart). Set mold in shallow pan of hot water. Bake in moderate oven (375° F.) thirty minutes. Turn out on warmed platter. Fill center with creamed mixed vegetables such as peas and carrots, or small Lima beans and corn. 4 to 6 servings.

For Parmesan Tuna Ring *use drained, flaked tuna fish.*

MENU

SHERRIED BROILED GRAPEFRUIT
PARMESAN CHICKEN RING
CREAMED LIMA BEANS AND CORN   WHOLE-WHEAT BREAD
PRUNE-AND-RAISIN PIE   COFFEE

RIO CHICKEN WITH RICE

Large frying chicken, cut in serving pieces
Salt and pepper
⅓ cup olive oil
2 cups rice
1 Spanish onion, peeled and chopped
1 green pepper, chopped
2 cloves garlic, peeled and chopped
1¼ teaspoons saffron
2 cups bouillon
2 cans (20-ounce) tomatoes
½ teaspoon paprika

Season chicken with salt and pepper; sauté in oil in heavy frying pan twenty minutes, or until lightly browned. Remove chicken to three-quart casserole. Sauté raw rice in the fat in frying pan until golden. Add onion, green pepper, and garlic and cook ten minutes. Stir in saffron mixed with one-fourth cup warm bouillon; add remaining bouillon, tomatoes, and paprika. Stir and heat together five minutes. Pour over chicken in casserole. Cover; bake in moderately-hot oven (400° F.) thirty minutes. Uncover and bake forty minutes longer, or until chicken is done. 4 to 6 servings.

In Spain, cooks use more saffron and garlic in this dish.

MENU

RIO CHICKEN WITH RICE
CHUTNEY WATERMELON PICKLE
BROILED EGGPLANT
HOT COMPOTE BLACK CHERRIES
(FLAVORED WITH KIRSCH)
COFFEE

SAFFRON-BASTED CHICKEN

Plump frying chicken, cut in serving pieces
2 teaspoons salt
½ teaspoon pepper
½ cup flour
4 tablespoons butter or margarine
½ teaspoon saffron, stirred into
¼ cup warm water
¼ cup lemon juice
Melted butter or margarine
¼ cup seedless raisins, soaked and drained
¼ teaspoon each thyme and orégano
½ teaspoon rosemary

Place chicken in paper bag with salt, pepper, and flour. Close tightly and shake to thoroughly coat chicken. Brown chicken in hot butter or margarine, in flameproof (metal-base) casserole, twenty minutes. Spoon extra fat from the dish; mix with saffron, water, lemon juice, melted butter or margarine, and baste chicken. Add raisins. Bake in moderate oven (375° F.) twenty-five minutes, or until chicken is done. Baste three or four times during baking period with the mixture of saffron, water, lemon juice and melted butter. Sprinkle with mixed herbs. Serve at once. 6 servings.

Rice and Major Grey's chutney good with this dish.

MENU

HOT TOMATO BOUILLON
TOASTED THIN SLICES SMALL RYE LOAF
SAFFRON-BASTED CHICKEN WILD RICE
CREAMED ONIONS
JELLY LAYER CAKE COFFEE

SANTA FÉ CHICKEN WITH FRUIT

1 plump roasting chicken, cut in serving pieces
Salt and cayenne
3 tablespoons fat or margarine
¾ cup chopped toasted almonds
½ cup seedless raisins
1 cup chopped canned pineapple
⅛ teaspoon cinnamon
⅛ teaspoon cloves
2 cups orange juice
2 oranges, peeled and sectioned

Season chicken; brown in fat in flameproof (metal-base) casserole (two-quart) fifteen minutes or until golden. Add almonds, raisins, pineapple, spices, and orange juice. Cover; cook in moderate oven (350° F.) fifty minutes, or until chicken is done. Baste frequently with juices in casserole. Add orange sections for last ten minutes of baking; uncover dish, and let chicken brown. 6 servings.

Mexican cooks add a light sprinkling of paprika to chicken and oranges.

MENU

SANTA FÉ CHICKEN WITH FRUIT
BAKED ACORN SQUASH
WATER-CRESS SALAD VINAIGRETTE DRESSING
GINGERBREAD VANILLA ICE CREAM
COFFEE

COD STEAKS

½ cup chopped peeled onion
3 tablespoons butter or margarine
2 tablespoons crumbs
Salt and pepper
4 medium-sized cod steaks
Juice ½ lemon
1 teaspoon capers
½ cup dry white wine
½ cup bouillon

Sauté onion in butter or margarine, in flameproof baking dish. When onions are golden, stir in crumbs. Cook five minutes. Push onions and crumbs aside. Season fish lightly; sauté three minutes on each side. Spoon onions and crumbs under and around cod, but not on top. Squeeze lemon juice over fish; add capers; mix wine and bouillon and add to dish. Cover. Bake in moderate oven (350° F.) twenty minutes; uncover, and continue baking five or ten minutes longer, until fish is done. 4 servings.

For Salmon Steaks *follow same recipe.*

MENU

FRENCH ONION SOUP
TOASTED FRENCH BREAD
COD STEAKS
BUTTERED BROCCOLI
CRANBERRY TURNOVER
SHARP CHEDDAR CHEESE
COFFEE

DEVILED CRAB, PRUNIER

2 pounds fresh, canned, or quick-frozen crab meat
2 tablespoons butter or margarine
2 tablespoons chopped peeled onion
2 shallots, peeled and chopped
1 tablespoon cognac
1 teaspoon Dijon or English mustard
1 cup well-seasoned medium white sauce
2 egg yolks
Mayonnaise
6 rounds thin toast, buttered
Paprika

Remove all bones and fibers from crab meat. Break up large chunks. Heat butter or margarine to foaming in saucepan; lightly sauté onion and shallots, five minutes. Remove onion and shallots, and discard. Add cognac to pan and tilt to blend with fat; stir in mustard, white sauce, beaten yolks, and one-fourth cup mayonnaise. Mix; add crab meat, and stir only to coat crab meat. Place toast in shallow baking dish. Spoon crab mixture generously over toast rounds. Top each with spoonful of mayonnaise. Sprinkle lightly with paprika. Bake in moderately-hot oven (400° F.) twenty to twenty-five minutes. 6 servings.

Never mind the calories; this isn't eaten every day.

MENU

GREEN PEPPER CHEESE RINGS
(GREEN PEPPERS STUFFED WITH CHEESE SPREAD, CHILLED, SLICED)
DEVILED CRAB, PRUNIER
ASPARAGUS WITH BROWNED CRUMBS
CRUSTY FRENCH ROLLS
LEMON SHERBET MADELEINES
COFFEE

FISH FILLETS AMANDINE

1½ pounds fish fillets (flounder preferred)
½ teaspoon salt
1 teaspoon curry powder
Butter or margarine
¾ teaspoon anchovy paste
½ cup chopped toasted almonds
1 tablespoon chopped capers
¾ cup chicken bouillon or consommé
4 tablespoons buttered crumbs
Lemon slices

Spread fillets in buttered shallow baking dish. Season with salt and curry powder. Cream one tablespoon butter or margarine and mix with anchovy paste; spread over fillets. Add a little melted butter or margarine to the dish. Bake in moderate oven (325° F.) twenty minutes, basting twice with melted butter or margarine. Mix almonds, capers, and bouillon or consommé; simmer five minutes. Pour over fish slowly; sprinkle top with buttered crumbs. Bake (350° F.) fifteen minutes longer, or until browned. Garnish dish with sliced lemon. 4 or 5 servings.

Thin fish steaks are delicious prepared by this recipe.

MENU

JELLIED TOMATO BOUILLON
FISH FILLETS AMANDINE
CREAMED POTATOES
CUCUMBER AND LETTUCE SALAD LEMON FRENCH DRESSING
CRUSTY FRENCH BREAD
APRICOT MOUSSE COFFEE

DUCK WITH COGNAC SAUCE

6-pound duckling, cut in serving pieces
Salt and pepper
2 red Spanish onions, peeled and chopped
3 sprigs parsley, chopped
½ bay leaf
¼ teaspoon thyme
Small sliver garlic, peeled and chopped
½ cup cognac
2 cups Burgundy or claret
¼ cup olive oil
½ pound mushrooms, peeled and sliced

Place duck in deep glass or pottery bowl. Sprinkle lightly with salt and pepper. Cover with onions, parsley, herbs, and garlic; pour cognac and wine over. Cover and let stand in refrigerator four hours. Drain duck, saving marinade. Heat oil in flameproof (metal-base) casserole; brown duck, turning all sides, about twelve minutes. Add marinade and mushrooms. Cover. Bake in moderate oven (350° F.) one hour, or until duck is done. Baste with mixture in baking dish. 4 to 6 servings.

A dish famous in the countryside near Rome.

MENU

SMOKED TROUT CANAPÉS COCKTAILS
DUCK WITH COGNAC SAUCE
TINY CRESCENT ROLLS
GRAPEFRUIT SALAD ORANGE FRENCH DRESSING
BROWN-SUGAR MERINGUES WITH CHOCOLATE ICE CREAM
COFFEE

SAVORY BRAISED DUCKLING

1 Long Island duckling, quartered
2 tablespoons butter or margarine
1 green pepper, chopped
1 onion, peeled and chopped
1 carrot, scraped and chopped
1 stalk celery, sliced
2 sprigs parsley
½ bay leaf
2 tablespoons cornstarch
Juice 1 lemon
1½ cups consommé
6 anchovy fillets, chopped
½ cup Madeira or sherry

Skin duckling. Melt butter or margarine in flameproof (metal-base) casserole. Brown duck over moderate heat. Add vegetables and cook about three minutes. Add parsley and bay leaf. Cover; cook in moderate oven (325° F.) forty-five minutes, or until duck is tender. Remove duck from casserole; discard vegetables, parsley, and bay leaf, and pour off excess fat. Stir cornstarch and lemon juice into remaining fat. When smooth, stir in consommé and anchovies. Cook, stirring until thickened. Return duck to casserole, spooning sauce over and around duck. Return to oven for ten minutes. Stir wine into sauce, spooning mixture over duck. 4 servings.

Prepare Savory Braised Chicken, *or* Turkey *by the same recipe; use small broiling turkey.*

MENU

SAVORY BRAISED DUCKLING
POTATOES AU GRATIN BUTTERED ARTICHOKE HEARTS
SMALL DINNER ROLLS
COMPOTE APRICOTS AND BLACK CHERRIES, FLAMBÉ COFFEE

FILLET OF FLOUNDER, CHEZ NOUS

(FLORENCE AND PETER GREIG, NEW YORK)

6 fillets of flounder
1 tablespoon prepared mustard
1 teaspoon dry mustard
2 tablespoons flour
½ teaspoon salt
½ teaspoon pepper
1 tablespoon French olive oil
1 tablespoon butter or margarine
⅜ cup heavy cream
2 tablespoons bread crumbs
2 tablespoons grated Parmesan cheese

Rinse fillets, wipe dry. Spread prepared mustard on one side of fillets. Combine dry mustard, flour, salt, and pepper; coat fish lightly. Heat oil in flameproof casserole (one and one-half quart); place fillets in hot oil, dot with butter or margarine; pour cream over; sprinkle with crumbs and cheese. Bake uncovered in preheated moderate oven (350° F.) thirty minutes. Place under moderate broiler heat five minutes; serve at once. 4 servings.

Also a good way to prepare cod or salmon steaks.

MENU

COCKTAILS RADISHES CARROT STICKS
CRISP COCKTAIL CRACKERS
FILLET OF FLOUNDER, CHEZ NOUS
MASHED POTATO PUFF *
BROWN-AND-SERVE WHOLE-WHEAT ROLLS
LEMON MERINGUE PIE COFFEE

OVEN GOULASH

1 pound each boned veal, lamb, and fresh pork
1 large onion, peeled and sliced
3 tablespoons shortening or margarine
3 tablespoons flour
1½ teaspoons salt
3 peppercorns
1 teaspoon paprika, about
¼ teaspoon nutmeg
3 whole cloves
½ bay leaf
1 cup dry white wine
2 cups bouillon or stock, about
1 cup light cream
1 package (8-ounce) noodles

Cut meat in one and one-half inch pieces. Cook onion until tender in fat in deep flameproof casserole (three-quart). Add meat, stir, and cook fifteen minutes. Sprinkle with flour, stirring to coat well. Add seasonings, wine, and bouillon or stock. Bring to boiling and boil five minutes. Stir in cream, and additional bouillon if needed. Liquid should barely cover meat. Cover casserole; bake in moderately-low oven (300° F.) one and one-half hours, or until meat is done and liquid has cooked down to thick sauce. Stir frequently during cooking.

When meat is nearly done, cook noodles as described on package. Drain. To serve, uncover casserole; make ring of cooked noodles on top of goulash. Sprinkle lightly with paprika. 6 to 8 servings.

Cream and pork may be omitted for simpler goulash.

MENU

OVEN GOULASH LIMA BEANS WITH LEMON BUTTER
SMALL CRESCENT ROLLS
MACEDOINE OF FRUIT
(FRUITS AND BERRIES IN SEASON WITH SHERRY) COFFEE

CRUMBED HAM SLICE

2-pound slice smoked ham
1½ cups coarse bread crumbs
2 tablespoons butter or margarine, melted
1½ teaspoons anchovy paste

Trim skin from ham; wipe meat with wet cloth. Cut fat in several places to prevent curling. Pan broil in (metal-base) flameproof baking dish, turning occasionally. When tender and lightly browned, about twenty minutes, cover with crumbs mixed with butter or margarine and anchovy paste. Place under moderate broiler heat to brown the crumbs, or in hot oven (450° F.) to brown fifteen minutes. Serve at once. 6 servings.

A *delicious variation: substitute chopped almonds for anchovy.*

MENU

CRUMBED HAM SLICE MASHED CARROTS
AVOCADO SALAD FRENCH DRESSING
(RIPE OLIVES, GRAPEFRUIT, GREEN PEPPER)
ITALIAN BREAD
PECAN PEARS * COFFEE

HAM FOR FOUR

2-pound slice ham
1 can (20-ounce) tomatoes, sieved
1 tablespoon prepared mustard
1 teaspoon A.1. sauce
1 tablespoon brown sugar
2 tablespoons sherry
1 green pepper, cut in thin rings
¼ cup chopped peeled onion
¼ cup chopped parsley

Cook ham ten minutes in flameproof (metal-base) baking dish, until lightly browned on both sides. Cut in serving pieces. Mix tomatoes, seasonings, and sherry, and pour over ham. Add green pepper, onion, and parsley. Cover, and cook in moderate oven (350° F.) until vegetables are done, about twenty-five minutes. Uncover dish, and let cook an additional five minutes. 4 servings.

With plain boiled potatoes, a man's dish for sure.

MENU

HAM FOR FOUR
NEW POTATOES IN JACKETS
BUTTERED GREEN BEANS
WHOLE-WHEAT BREAD CURRANT JELLY
APPLE PIE
BRIE OR CHEDDAR CHEESE
ALE OR BEER COFFEE

SMOTHERED LAMB CHOPS

6 rib lamb chops
Salt and pepper
2 tablespoons butter or margarine
5 medium-sized potatoes
3 large onions, peeled and sliced thin
1½ cups bouillon or consommé (about)
2 tablespoons minced parsley
4 tablespoons buttered bread crumbs

Wipe chops with wet cloth. Season lightly with salt and pepper. Sauté in butter or margarine in flameproof (metal-base) baking dish. Cover dish and cook ten minutes, or until meat is lightly browned on all sides. Scrub potatoes; drain, pare, and slice thin over chops. Spread onions over potatoes. Season lightly with salt. Cover with bouillon or consommé. Cover casserole. Bake in moderate oven (375° F.) thirty-five minutes, or until vegetables are cooked and meat done. Add more consommé if needed. Sprinkle parsley and buttered crumbs over top. Turn oven to hot (450° F.). Continue to bake, uncovered ten minutes, or until crumbs are lightly browned. 6 servings.

For Smothered Veal Chops, *substitute veal for lamb.*

MENU

MIXED VEGETABLE JUICE HOT CHEESE CANAPÉS
SMOTHERED LAMB CHOPS
TOMATO ASPIC ON ESCAROLE FRENCH DRESSING
CARAMEL CUPCAKES
COFFEE-AND-COGNAC FLAMBÉ

CURRIED ROCK LOBSTER TAILS

4 lobster tails (about 6-ounces each)
Juice ½ lemon
5 tablespoons butter or margarine
2 tablespoons flour
1½ teaspoons curry powder
¼ teaspoon celery salt
⅛ teaspoon nutmeg
1 cup milk
½ cup light cream

If quick-frozen lobster tails are used, defrost according to package directions. If fresh tails are used, cover with boiling salted water and boil nine minutes. Drain; cover with cold water. When cool, drain again. Cut under shell with scissors, and pull out meat. Cut in bite-size pieces; sprinkle with lemon juice. Melt four tablespoons butter or margarine in saucepan; stir flour in smoothly; add one teaspoon curry powder, the celery salt, and nutmeg. Add milk and cream, slowly, stirring until smooth and slightly thickened. Remove from heat. In shallow flameproof (metal-base) baking dish, heat remaining tablespoon butter or margarine; stir remaining curry powder into it; when very hot, add lobster meat, stir only enough to coat with butter and curry. Pour curry sauce over. Place in hot oven (425° F.) and heat five minutes, or until bubbly. 4 servings.

An easily doubled recipe for a Friday night buffet party.

MENU

TIO PEPE DRY SHERRY
ANCHOVY AND CREAM CHEESE ON PUMPERNICKEL
RIPE OLIVES CHUTNEY CHOPPED GREEN PEPPER
CURRIED ROCK LOBSTER TAILS SAFFRON RICE
TOASTED ROLLS BLACK CURRANT JAM
PLUM TART COFFEE

LOBSTER IMPERIAL

1 can (4-ounce) mushrooms
2 tablespoons chopped green pepper
2 tablespoons chopped peeled onion
3 tablespoons butter or margarine
2 cups fresh, canned, or quick-frozen lobster meat (defrosted)
2 tablespoons chopped pimiento
1 teaspoon dry mustard
¼ teaspoon pepper
1 egg
⅔ cup mayonnaise
2 slices bread
Paprika

Drain mushrooms; slice or chop. Cook green pepper and onion in one tablespoon butter or margarine, five minutes. Combine with lobster. Add pimiento and seasonings. Beat egg, combine with mayonnaise, and pour over. Mix well. Pour into greased shallow baking dish (one-quart). Cut six small rounds from bread slices; sauté in remaining two tablespoons butter or margarine. Lay rounds on top of lobster mixture. Add light sprinkling of paprika to dish. Bake in moderate oven (350° F.) twenty minutes, or until bubbly. 6 servings.

Doubled, this recipe makes a good buffet-party dish.

MENU

FRESH FRUIT CUP
(PEAR, RED RASPBERRIES, HONEYDEW MELON)
LOBSTER IMPERIAL TINY FRENCH PEAS
RUM OR SHERRY CAKE COFFEE

SCALLOPED OYSTERS

2 dozen shelled oysters
2 cups bread crumbs
6 tablespoons butter or margarine
Salt and pepper
⅛ teaspoon nutmeg
¼ teaspoon celery salt
¾ cup light cream
½ cup oyster liquor

If quick-frozen oysters are used, defrost according to directions. Drain fresh or defrosted oysters; save one-half cup liquor. Remove all shell particles. Make layer of crumbs in buttered casserole (one and one-half quart); dot with butter or margarine. Cover with oysters; season lightly with salt and pepper. Repeat layers, making top layer crumbs. Mix nutmeg and celery salt with cream and oyster liquor; pour over contents of dish. Dot with butter. Bake in moderate oven (375° F.) fifteen minutes, or until brown. 6 servings.

Easily doubled for buffet and barbecue parties.

MENU

COCKTAILS STUFFED CELERY POTATO CHIPS
SCALLOPED OYSTERS
BAKED STUFFED TOMATOES
BROWN-AND-SERVE DINNER ROLLS
WARM PEACH TURNOVERS GOUDA CHEESE
ALE OR BEER COFFEE

OVEN-COOKED PEAS AND SCALLIONS

1 pound fresh peas, or
  1 package quick-frozen, defrosted
6 young scallions
½ teaspoon salt
⅛ teaspoon pepper
1 tablespoon sugar
2 tablespoons butter or margarine
1 teaspoon flour
¾ cup boiling consommé or water
1 tablespoon mixed fresh parsley, chives, and dried chervil

Wash and shell peas. Wash scallions; cut off root end and all green; slice white part thin. Combine with peas in casserole (one-quart). Add salt, pepper, and sugar. Mix butter or margarine and flour; add consommé or water and mix smoothly. Stir into peas and scallions. Cover. Cook in moderate oven (375° F.) about thirty minutes, until peas are done. Stir herbs in. 3 or 4 servings.

Easily cooked while another oven dish is baking.

MENU

PINEAPPLE JUICE CHIVE-CHEESE CRACKERS
ROAST LEG OF LAMB
OVEN-COOKED PEAS AND SCALLIONS
CRACKED-WHEAT BREAD CURRANT JELLY
CARAMEL LAYER CAKE
COFFEE

PORK PIE WITH PASTRY TOP

(MABEL STEGNER, NEW YORK)

3 cups cubed cooked pork
3 cups sliced carrots
3 tablespoons fat
¼ cup chopped peeled onion
3 tablespoons flour
1½ cups well-seasoned chicken broth
½ teaspoon Kitchen Bouquet
¼ teaspoon ginger
⅛ teaspoon dry mustard
1 teaspoon salt
1 cup chopped green peppers
1/16 teaspoon thyme
½ package pastry-mix

Cut pork in small cubes. Cook carrots until barely tender in small amount of boiling salted water. Melt fat over moderate heat. Add onion and cook one minute. Stir in flour. Add chicken broth and cook, stirring frequently, until sauce thickens. Add Kitchen Bouquet, ginger, mustard, and salt. Combine sauce, pork, carrots, and green peppers. Pour into greased shallow baking dish (two-quart). Keep in warm place while preparing pastry for topping. Add thyme to pastry-mix; add water according to directions on package. Roll pastry out on lightly-floured board in shape to fit top of baking dish; cut vents to allow escape of steam. Place topping on pie. Bake in moderately-hot oven (400° F.) until pastry is lightly browned, about twenty-five minutes. Serve immediately. 4 to 6 servings.

Such good flavor and a gem for a low-budget dinner.

MENU

TOMATO JUICE CELERY CRACKERS
PORK PIE WITH PASTRY TOP
FRUIT SALAD
(CANTALOUPE RING WITH SEEDLESS GRAPES AND BLUEBERRIES)
MADELEINES COFFEE

BOUILLON-BAKED POTATOES

4 medium-sized potatoes
2 tablespoons butter or margarine
2 tablespoons flour
2 cups bouillon or stock (about)
1 onion, peeled
2 whole cloves
Sprig parsley
Salt and pepper
½ teaspoon marjoram
¼ teaspoon basil

Scrub potatoes, pare, and slice. Melt butter or margarine in flameproof baking dish (one and one-half quart). Stir flour smoothly in; add bouillon or stock, and cook stirring until slightly thickened. Add onion with cloves stuck in it, and parsley. Add potatoes. Liquid should cover potatoes; add more bouillon if needed. Season with salt and pepper. Cook uncovered in moderate oven (350° F.) twenty-five minutes. Sprinkle herbs over potatoes, and continue baking until potatoes are done and liquid soaked up. Baste during cooking two or three times. Serve very hot. 4 servings.

Even calory counters ask for second helpings of this dish.

MENU

BROILED VEAL CHOPS
BOUILLON-BAKED POTATOES
PETITS POIS
(CANNED TINY FRENCH PEAS IN BUTTER)
ASSORTED BREADS
BAKED STUFFED PEACHES *
COFFEE

DREAM STREET SCALLOPED POTATOES

4 boiled potatoes, sliced thin
1 teaspoon salt
1 tablespoon butter or margarine
2 hard-cooked eggs, sliced
1 cup sour cream
¼ cup chopped cooked ham
½ cup light cream
½ cup buttered crumbs

Arrange half the potato slices in a greased baking dish (one and one-half quart). Season lightly with salt and dabs of butter or margarine. Cover with egg slices. Pour half the sour cream over the eggs. Add remaining potato slices; cover with ham. Add remaining sour cream mixed with light cream and buttered crumbs. Bake in hot oven (450° F.) thirty minutes, or until top is browned. 4 servings.

Delicious, too, when chopped sardines replace the ham.

MENU

SPLIT-PEA SOUP
TOASTED FRENCH BREAD
DREAM STREET SCALLOPED POTATOES
LEMON-ASPIC FRUIT SALAD
(MIXED CANNED OR FRESH FRUITS)
WHIPPED-CREAM MAYONNAISE
COFFEE

SCALLOPS WITH MUSHROOMS

2 pounds small scallops
Juice 1 lemon
4 tablespoons butter or margarine
1 small onion, peeled and chopped
3 tablespoons flour
¼ teaspoon celery salt
¼ teaspoon thyme
1 teaspoon salt
½ teaspoon Worcestershire sauce
1 can (6-ounce) broiled mushrooms
¼ cup sherry or Madeira
½ cup buttered crumbs

If scallops are large, slice crosswise. If quick-frozen scallops are used, defrost according to directions on package. Wash scallops, drain; cover with water and add lemon juice. Boil three minutes. Drain, saving one and one-half cups liquid.

Melt butter or margarine in a saucepan; sauté onion ten minutes, or until soft. Add flour and seasonings, and mix well. Add liquid from scallops, stirring until smooth and thickened. Add scallops, mushrooms, and wine. Mix, and pour into buttered baking dish (two-quart); cover with crumbs. Bake in moderate oven (350° F.) fifteen minutes. 6 servings.

Another buffet favorite when recipe is doubled. Serve with tartare sauce.

MENU

MIXED CLAM AND TOMATO JUICE
CHEESE STRAWS
SCALLOPS WITH MUSHROOMS
POTATOES, PARSLEY BUTTER
BROWN-AND-SERVE DINNER ROLLS
MELON COFFEE

CRUMBED SCALLOPS

2 pounds small scallops
Juice 1 lemon
2 cups fine bread crumbs
1 teaspoon salt
½ teaspoon pepper
¼ teaspoon celery salt
½ teaspoon paprika
2 eggs
½ cup water
6 slices bacon

If quick-frozen scallops are used, defrost according to directions on package. Wash scallops; drain; cover with boiling water; add lemon juice. Boil three minutes. Drain; if large, slice crosswise. Roll scallops in crumbs mixed with seasonings. Dip in beaten eggs mixed with water; then in crumbs again. Place scallops in greased baking dish (two-quart); cover with strips of bacon. Bake in moderately-hot oven (400° F.) fifteen minutes, or until bacon is brown. Serve with lemon wedges, chili sauce, or tartare sauce. 6 servings.

For Crumbed Shrimp *substitute quick-frozen shrimp.*

MENU

CREAM OF TOMATO SOUP
TOASTED SLICES SMALL RYE LOAF
CRUMBED SCALLOPS
LEMON WEDGES TARTARE SAUCE
MIXED FRUITS IN WINE JELLY COLD CUSTARD SAUCE *
COFFEE

BOSTON SCROD WITH HERBED TOMATOES

2 pounds sliced scrod
4 tablespoons butter or margarine
1 can (20-ounce) tomatoes, sieved
1 teaspoon sugar
1½ teaspoons salt
¼ teaspoon pepper
½ teaspoon orégano
1 medium-sized onion, peeled and chopped
2 tablespoons chopped green pepper
¼ cup bread crumbs

Wipe fish with wet cloth. Cut scrod in serving pieces; place in greased baking dish. Dot with one tablespoon butter or margarine. Combine tomatoes with seasonings, onion, and green pepper, and pour over fish. Stir crumbs in one tablespoon butter or margarine to coat them, and brown slightly. Sprinkle crumbs over fish, dot with remaining butter or margarine. Bake, uncovered, in moderately-hot oven (400° F.) thirty minutes. 4 servings.

Any fish fillets or steaks may be used in place of scrod.

MENU

SHRIMP IN TARTARE SAUCE
BOSTON SCROD WITH HERBED TOMATOES
FRENCH-FRIED ONIONS
MASHED POTATOES AU GRATIN
CORN BREAD   APPLE BUTTER
CHOCOLATE CHIFFON PIE   COFFEE

BASKERVILLE SHAD ROE

2 large shad roe, or
 4 small roe
1 cup bread crumbs
3 tablespoons butter or margarine
3 cups thick white sauce
1 cup light cream
¼ teaspoon celery salt
¼ teaspoon onion salt
¼ cup Madeira
Toast triangles

Rinse roe; cover with boiling water; simmer ten minutes. Drain; cover with cold water and let stand five minutes. Drain; remove skin; use fork to separate into serving pieces. Place in buttered shallow baking dish. Sauté crumbs in butter or margarine until lightly browned. Cover roe with half the crumbs. Combine white sauce, cream, and seasonings. Heat, stirring until blended; add wine, stir, and remove from heat. Pour over roe; sprinkle with remaining buttered crumbs. Bake in moderate oven (375° F.) until sauce is bubbling around the roe, about twenty minutes. Serve on toast triangles. 4 servings.

If canned roe is used, no pre-boiling is necessary.

MENU

JELLIED MADRILÈNE
BASKERVILLE SHAD ROE
SMALL NEW POTATOES, PARSLEY BUTTER
BUTTERED ASPARAGUS
TOASTED SMALL ROLLS BLACKBERRY JAM
PEACH-AND-APPLE DESSERT *
COFFEE

BALTIMORE FILLETS OF SOLE

1 pound fillets of sole
½ cup bread or cracker crumbs
8 cooked shrimp, cleaned
2 tablespoons butter or margarine
½ cup curry sauce
¼ cup heavy cream, whipped

Rinse fish in slightly-salted water; drain; let stand a few minutes. Arrange fillets in lightly-buttered shallow baking dish. Sauté crumbs and the shrimp in the butter or margarine until crumbs are browned. Place shrimp and half of the crumbs over the fish. Combine curry sauce and cream, pour over the top. Sprinkle with remaining crumbs. Bake in a hot oven (475° F.) fifteen minutes.

For Baltimore Fillets of Halibut *or other mild fish, follow this recipe.*

MENU

COLESLAW APPETIZER
(COLESLAW, CHOPPED PICKLE, RUSSIAN DRESSING)
BALTIMORE FILLETS OF SOLE
MACARONI SHELLS AU GRATIN
BROWN BREAD PEACH BUTTER
WATERMELON
COFFEE

OVEN-FRIED TURKEY

4- to 6-pound fryer turkey, cut in serving pieces
½ cup flour
1½ teaspoons salt
½ teaspoon each: pepper, paprika, celery salt, garlic salt
1 teaspoon orégano
Fat
4 tablespoons butter or margarine, melted
¼ cup bouillon
¼ cup dry white wine

Place pieces of turkey in a paper bag. Mix flour, seasonings, and herb. Shake in tightly-closed bag until turkey is well coated. Brown seasoned turkey in one-half inch hot fat in a heavy frying pan. Arrange one-layer deep in large shallow (metal-base) casserole. Add butter or margarine, bouillon, and wine. Cover; bake in moderate oven (350° F.) thirty minutes. Uncover and continue baking another half hour, until turkey is crisply browned. 6 servings.

Good cold, too, for picnic lunch the next day.

MENU

CREAM OF CELERY SOUP MELBA TOAST
OVEN-FRIED TURKEY
BUTTERED ZUCCHINI BAKED SWEET POTATOES
DINNER ROLLS
SMALL CHERRY-AND-ORANGE TARTS
COFFEE

STUFFED VEAL, ITALIAN STYLE

1½ pounds veal cutlet, in
 1 or 2 large slices
Salt and pepper
¼ pound prosciutto or baked ham
1 clove garlic, peeled and chopped
2 tablespoons chopped parsley
1 large onion, peeled and chopped
5 tablespoons olive oil
1 can (17-ounce) tomatoes, sieved
½ teaspoon basil

Wipe meat with wet cloth. Season well with salt and pepper. Chop or grind prosciutto or ham; combine with garlic, parsley, and onion. Spread mixture on veal. Roll carefully; fasten roll with wooden picks or skewers. Brown quickly in oil in flameproof shallow baking dish, about five minutes on each side. Add tomatoes. Cover. Bake in moderate oven (350° F.) forty-five minutes to one hour. Add basil for last fifteen minutes. Remove skewers before taking dish to table. 4 to 6 servings.

Oven-browned potatoes or saffron rice delicious with this.

MENU

TIO PEPE DRY SHERRY
CELERY HEARTS CARROT STICKS
STUFFED VEAL, ITALIAN STYLE
OVEN-BROWNED POTATOES
CRUSTY BREAD
COFFEE CUSTARD SPONGECAKE
COFFEE

BAKED VEAL PARMIGIANA

2 eggs
1 teaspoon salt
½ teaspoon pepper
1 cup bread crumbs
3 tablespoons grated Parmesan cheese
1½ pounds thin veal cutlet
6 tablespoons olive oil
2 cans (10½-ounce) condensed tomato soup
½ pound Mozzarella cheese

Beat eggs well; add salt and pepper. Mix crumbs and Parmesan. Wipe veal with wet cloth. Dip cutlets in egg, then into crumbs. Sauté in hot oil in shallow flameproof casserole five minutes on each side. Pour tomato soup over cutlets. Cover with thin slices of Mozzarella. Bake in moderately-low oven (300° F.) twenty minutes, or until sauce is bubbly and cheese turns light brown. Serve very hot. 4 servings.

Italian Chianti wine is just right with this dish.

MENU

ANTIPASTO
(SARDINES, CELERY, PIMIENTO, RIPE OLIVES)
BAKED VEAL PARMIGIANA
CHIANTI
SPAGHETTI WITH BUTTER SAUCE BUTTERED ZUCCHINI
SPUMONI MACAROONS
COFFEE

GUEST DINNER VEAL BIRDS

2 pounds veal cutlet
Salt and pepper
1 cup bread crumbs
4 tablespoons butter or margarine
¼ cup chopped ripe olives
2 tablespoons each: chopped parsley, lemon peel
1 teaspoon mixed dried marjoram, basil, thyme
¼ cup fine cracker crumbs
1 cup each: bouillon, dry white wine

Have butcher cut veal in slices one-fourth inch thick as for scaloppine. Wipe meat with wet cloth; cut six oblong pieces equal in shape and size. Pound meat well; season with salt and pepper. Mix crumbs, two tablespoons melted butter or margarine, the olives, parsley, lemon peel, and herbs. Place a generous spoonful of filling on one end of each meat slice. Roll up carefully, tucking in the ends as you roll. Fasten with wooden pick. Roll each in cracker crumbs; sauté in flameproof (metal-base) baking dish using remaining two tablespoons butter or margarine. When lightly browned on all sides, add bouillon and wine to dish. Cover and place in moderate oven (350° F.). Bake twenty-five minutes. Remove cover; baste with sauce in dish. Bake fifteen minutes uncovered. Remove wooden picks. 6 servings.

Makes a good buffet-supper main dish, too.

MENU

HONEYDEW MELON
GUEST DINNER VEAL BIRDS
CREAMED ONIONS BROCCOLI WITH CRUMBS
POPPY-SEED ROLLS BLACKBERRY JELLY SLICED PICKLES
FRUITCAKE
GRAND MARNIER COFFEE

VEAL CHOPS WITH ANCHOVIES

4 veal chops
1 teaspoon salt
½ teaspoon pepper
¼ cup flour
4 tablespoons butter or margarine
4 anchovy fillets
1 cup light cream
1 cup sour cream
Paprika
White wine, if required

Wipe chops with wet cloth. Dip meat in seasoned flour. Brown lightly in butter or margarine in shallow flameproof casserole. Place anchovy on each chop. Mix cream and sour cream, and pour over chops. Sprinkle lightly with paprika. Bake in moderate oven (350° F.) thirty-five minutes, or until meat is done. If additional liquid is needed during baking, stir a little white wine into the pan juices, and baste the chops. 4 servings.

For Chicken Breasts with Anchovies, *use split chicken breasts.*

MENU

COCKTAILS DEVILED EGGS RIPE OLIVES
VEAL CHOPS WITH ANCHOVIES
B&G SPARKLING BURGUNDY
PETITS POIS
(CANNED TINY FRENCH PEAS IN BUTTER)
NOODLES AU GRATIN
ROLLS
LINZER TORTE (OPEN-FACE RASPBERRY JAM PIE)
COFFEE

OVEN ZUCCHINI

4 small zucchini
2 tablespoons butter, or margarine, or
  2 strips bacon, chopped
1 teaspoon salt
½ teaspoon pepper
Paprika

Wash zucchini and drain; do not pare. Cut in halves lengthwise. Arrange in greased shallow baking dish. Dot with butter or margarine or sprinkle with pieces of bacon. Season with salt and pepper; and sprinkle lightly with paprika. Add one tablespoon water to bottom of baking dish. Cover, and bake fifteen minutes in moderately-hot oven (400° F.). Uncover and continue baking another ten minutes until tender. 4 servings.

Especially good with lamb and veal.

MENU

TOMATO JUICE   STUFFED CELERY
BROILED LAMB CHOPS   SPICED CRAB APPLES
OVEN ZUCCHINI   WILD RICE WITH MUSHROOMS
CURRANT JAM   SMALL DINNER ROLLS
MARBLE CAKE   COFFEE

a casserole supper
can be an occasion

CHEESE-PASTRY SALAMI PIE

Pastry-mix for 1 crust
¼ cup grated Old English cheese
1½ cups medium white sauce
½ tablespoon prepared mustard
1½ cups cubed salami
1 cup cooked peas, drained
1 green pepper, chopped fine
2 hard-cooked eggs, cubed

Prepare pastry according to package directions; work cheese into pastry and blend well. Roll out to fit top of baking dish about ten-by-six-by-two inches. Prick with fork. Mix white sauce and mustard; add salami, peas, green pepper, and eggs. Mix well. Pour into greased baking dish; cover with pastry; crimp edge of pastry to dish. Bake in hot oven (425° F.) twenty minutes, or until crust is golden brown. 6 servings.

Tastes fine with ale or beer for a club supper.

MENU

CHEESE-PASTRY SALAMI PIE
TOSSED LETTUCE AND RIPE OLIVE SALAD
FRENCH DRESSING
SWEETMEAT TRAY OF SALTED ALMONDS,
NOUGAT, DATES, STUFFED PRUNES
ALE BEER COFFEE

SUNDAY NIGHT CHEESE CASSEROLE

(RAY LEE JACKSON, COLUMBUS, OHIO)

6 slices bread
½ pound Old English cheese, sliced very thin
1 onion, peeled and chopped fine
2 teaspoons Worcestershire sauce
1½ teaspoons salt
1½ teaspoons dry mustard
1 teaspoon Accent
2½ cups milk
4 eggs

Cut crusts from bread. Place slices in buttered casserole (one and one-half quart). Cover with slices of cheese; scatter a little onion on the cheese. Repeat layers of bread, cheese, and onions. Add Worcestershire and seasonings to milk. Beat eggs and combine with milk, beating well. Pour over cheese- and bread-filled casserole. Cover, and let stand one to two hours in refrigerator. Remove from refrigerator twenty minutes before baking. Bake in moderate oven (325° F.) two hours. 6 servings. Best results with straight-sided casserole.

Easy on the hostess. Casserole is ready for oven long before guests arrive.

MENU

SUNDAY NIGHT CHEESE CASSEROLE
BAKED HAM
HOT BISCUITS
CHUTNEY MIXED OLIVES
APRICOT JAM TART
CHERRY HEERING CORDIAL COFFEE

QUICHE LORRAINE

Pastry-mix for 1 crust
8 slices bacon
½ pound Swiss or Gruyère cheese, sliced
4 eggs
1 tablespoon flour
½ teaspoon salt
½ teaspoon celery salt
¼ teaspoon cayenne
¼ teaspoon nutmeg
2 cups top milk
1 tablespoon butter, melted

Prepare pastry as described on package; line shallow baking dish or pie plate (nine-inch). Broil or pan-cook bacon until done but not crisp. Place four slices bacon in pastry shell; cover with cheese. Repeat bacon and cheese. Beat eggs; combine with flour, salt, and other seasonings, beating smooth. Add milk and butter. Mix; pour over cheese and bacon. Bake in moderate oven (375° F.) forty minutes or until custard is set. Serve warm. 6 servings.

Garnish with crisp bacon curls when you serve this as a main dish.

MENU

TOMATO JUICE WATER-CRESS CANAPÉS
QUICHE LORRAINE
MELON-RING FRUIT SALAD
(HONEYDEW MELON RING FILLED WITH SLICED PEACHES, CHERRIES, PLUMS)
HONEY FRENCH DRESSING
COFFEE MADELEINES

JACKSON'S CHICKEN DISH

(RAY LEE JACKSON, COLUMBUS, OHIO)

2 cups cubed cooked chicken
2 cups sliced celery
½ cup chopped or slivered almonds
2 tablespoons chopped peeled onion
2 tablespoons lemon juice
1 green pepper, chopped
1 teaspoon salt
1 cup mayonnaise
½ cup light cream
¾ cup crushed potato chips
2 tablespoons grated cheese
Paprika

Mix all ingredients but potato chips, cheese, and paprika. Pour into greased casserole (one and one-half quart). Cover with potato chips and grated cheese. Sprinkle with paprika. Bake in a moderate oven (350° F.) thirty minutes, or until browned. 6 servings.

Popular supper dish at the studio of this Ohio gourmet host.

MENU

CAVIAR CANAPÉS COCKTAILS
JACKSON'S CHICKEN DISH
TOMATO AND CHICORY SALAD FRENCH DRESSING
TOASTED CRACKERS
MERINGUE SHELLS WITH RED RASPBERRIES
COFFEE

CRAB-MEAT DELIGHT

(HELEN AND CHARLES HOVEY, NEW YORK)

6 tablespoons butter or margarine
2 tablespoons flour
2 cups light cream, scalded
¼ cup grated Swiss cheese
¼ cup grated Parmesan cheese
½ teaspoon salt
¼ teaspoon cayenne
2 cups cooked or canned crab meat, bones removed
Toast points

Melt two tablespoons butter or margarine in saucepan; stir flour in smoothly; add cream and cook, stirring until slightly thickened. Add cheeses; stir until melted. Add remaining butter or margarine, beating hard. Season with salt and cayenne. Arrange cleaned crab meat in buttered shallow baking dish (one-quart). Pour sauce over crab meat; place under moderately-hot broiler eight to ten minutes, until bubbly and golden brown. Serve on toast points. 6 to 8 servings.

For Lobster Delight *substitute cooked canned lobster meat.*

MENU

TOMATO JUICE SESAME-SEED CRACKERS
CRAB-MEAT DELIGHT
ENDIVE AND GRAPEFRUIT SALAD
LEMON-AND-SHERRY FRENCH DRESSING
PETITS FOURS
COFFEE

POTTED DUCK, CHINESE STYLE

3 tablespoons peanut oil
1 drop sesame oil
5-pound duckling, cut in serving pieces
1½ cups chopped canned water chestnuts
1½ cups chopped canned bamboo shoots
2 scallions, chopped fine
1 teaspoon shredded ginger root
1 can (3-ounce) chopped broiled mushrooms
1½ cups chopped celery
5 cups water
1 tablespoon cornstarch
3 tablespoons soy sauce
3 tablespoons sherry
1 teaspoon sugar

Heat the two oils in a deep flameproof, (metal-base) casserole (two-quart). Sauté duck seven minutes, or until lightly cooked. Add chestnuts, bamboo shoots, scallions, ginger root, mushrooms, celery, and water. Bring to boiling and boil three minutes. Cover; place in moderate oven (350° F.) and cook one and one-half hours. Add more liquid from time to time, if needed. Mix cornstarch, soy sauce, sherry, and sugar; stir into casserole. Cook uncovered until boiling and thickened. Serve with rice or thin noodles. 6 servings.

Assorted curry condiments are sometimes served with this dish.

MENU

POTTED DUCK, CHINESE STYLE HOT RICE
CHOPPED GREEN PEPPER CHOPPED PEANUTS
GRATED COCONUT CHUTNEY SHREDDED PINEAPPLE
BREAD-AND-BUTTER FINGER SANDWICHES
CARAMEL CAKE COFFEE

LOBSTER-STUFFED EGGS IN CURRY SAUCE

(JEANNE AND HOWARD SMITH, LANSDOWNE, PENNSYLVANIA)

4 hard-cooked eggs
2 tablespoons mayonnaise
1 tablespoon milk
½ teaspoon Better Products all-purpose seasoning
1 teaspoon lemon juice
1 cup cooked, canned, or quick-frozen lobster meat
2 slices bread, toasted and quartered
1 cup curry sauce *
½ cup grated Swiss cheese

Remove shells from eggs; cut in half lengthwise. Remove yolks and press through sieve. Add mayonnaise, milk, seasoning, and lemon juice to yolks and blend thoroughly. Add lobster meat. Heap mixture lightly into egg whites. Arrange toast in buttered baking dish; set stuffed eggs on toast. Pour curry sauce over all. Sprinkle with cheese; bake in moderate oven (375° F.) fifteen to twenty minutes. 4 servings.

For Shrimp-stuffed Eggs in Curry Sauce, *substitute chopped shrimp.*

MENU

LOBSTER-STUFFED EGGS IN CURRY SAUCE
GRAPEFRUIT, GREEN PEPPER, OLIVE SALAD
FRENCH DRESSING
PINEAPPLE SHERBET VANILLA WAFERS
COFFEE

EGGPLANT-LAMB CASSEROLE

(CHARLOTTE ADAMS, NEW YORK)

2 medium-sized eggplant
1 pound mushrooms
3 tablespoons butter or margarine
3/8 cup chopped peeled onions
1 clove garlic, peeled and crushed
1 tablespoon bacon fat
2 tablespoons flour
2 cups mushroom liquor
3/8 cup chopped sweet red pepper
2 cups diced cooked lamb
1 teaspoon orégano
Bread crumbs

Wash, pare, and dice eggplant. Cook fifteen minutes in boiling salted water to cover. Drain; mash. While eggplant cooks, wash, peel, and stem mushrooms. Cover stems and peelings with four cups water; boil slowly until liquid is reduced by half, about thirty minutes. Chop mushroom caps coarsely; sauté in two tablespoons butter or margarine five minutes. Sauté onions and garlic in bacon fat until lightly browned. Add flour; blend well. Add mushroom liquor, stirring until smooth and thick. Add eggplant, mushrooms, red pepper, lamb, orégano. Mix thoroughly; pile into buttered casserole (two-quart). Cover with crumbs; dot with remaining tablespoon of butter. Bake in moderately-hot oven (400° F.) thirty minutes. 6 servings.

The favorite casserole recipe of this famous gourmet-editor.

MENU

DRY SHERRY — CHEESE AND ANCHOVY CANAPÉS
SLICED TURKEY — CHUTNEY
EGGPLANT-LAMB CASSEROLE — CRUSTY FRENCH ROLLS, BUTTERED
BOMBE OF PISTACHIO ICE CREAM AND RASPBERRY SHERBET
SPICE CAKE — COFFEE

EGGPLANT VEGETABLE CASSEROLE

1 large eggplant
4 large onions, peeled and sliced
4 tablespoons butter or margarine
1 pound mushroom caps, fresh or canned
4 large tomatoes, peeled and chopped
2 green peppers, cut in strips
2 teaspoons salt
1 teaspoon pepper
¼ teaspoon basil
¼ teaspoon orégano
1 bay leaf
¼ cup buttered bread crumbs

Wash eggplant; pare; cut in one-inch slices. Cover with boiling water and boil fifteen minutes. Drain. Sauté onions in butter or margarine until browned. Add mushrooms and cook five minutes, or two minutes for canned mushrooms. Make layer of eggplant in a buttered casserole (two-quart). Add tomatoes, peppers, seasonings, and herbs to the mushrooms and onions. Pour over eggplant; cover with buttered crumbs. Bake in slow oven (275° F.) one and one-half hours. 8 servings.

Popular for buffet suppers any time of the year.

MENU

EGGPLANT VEGETABLE CASSEROLE
TOASTED BRIOCHE PLUM JAM
RUM CAKE COFFEE

FISH STICKS AU GRATIN

1 package quick-frozen fish sticks
1 cup medium white sauce
1 tablespoon cut chives
1 tablespoon lemon juice
3 tablespoons grated Cheddar cheese
Paprika

Place fish sticks in shallow baking dish. Combine white sauce, chives, lemon juice, and cheese. Pour over sticks. Sprinkle lightly with paprika. Bake in a hot oven (425° F.) twenty minutes, or until sauce is bubbly and browning. 4 servings.

A *quickie for unexpected guests, or for luncheon visitors.*

MENU

HONEYDEW MELON SEEDLESS GRAPES
FISH STICKS AU GRATIN
CORN MUFFINS
APPLE-RAISIN PIE
COFFEE

STUFFED FISH FILLETS

1½ pounds fish fillets
1 teaspoon salt
2 cups soft bread crumbs
Lemon juice
⅛ teaspoon pepper
¼ teaspoon celery salt
½ teaspoon curry powder
¼ cup chopped parsley
¼ cup melted butter or margarine (about)

Wipe fillets with wet cloth. Sprinkle with salt. Roll each fillet loosely and fasten with wooden pick. Arrange in greased shallow baking dish. Fill rings with stuffing made by mixing crumbs, two tablespoons lemon juice, pepper, celery salt, curry powder, and parsley. Moisten with a little melted butter or margarine. Brush stuffed fillet rings with remaining butter or margarine. Bake in hot oven (450° F.) fifteen to twenty minutes, or until fish is done. Baste once during baking with mixed lemon juice and melted butter or margarine. Remove wooden picks before serving. 6 servings.

Stuffing may be varied; add chopped pistachio nuts or hazel nuts.

MENU

STUFFED FISH FILLETS
SUCCOTASH
POPPY-SEED ROLLS
MINT SHERBET ON SLICED ORANGES
COFFEE

CALIFORNIA HAM CASSEROLE

1¼ cups rice
3 cups water
1½ teaspoons salt
¾ cup ripe olives
¾ cup thinly-sliced celery
¼ cup chopped peeled onions
2 tablespoons chopped green pepper
2 tablespoons oil
1 cup grated American cheese
⅔ cup cubed cooked ham

Rinse rice; drain. Add water and salt and heat to boiling. Cover tightly and cook twenty-five minutes over very low heat. Cut olives into large pieces. Cook celery, onions, and pepper in oil five minutes. Fluff up hot cooked rice with a fork; add olives, vegetables, cheese, and ham; mix lightly. Pile into six greased individual baking dishes. Bake in moderate oven (350° F.) ten minutes, or until cheese melts. 6 servings.

Ideal for tray supper, indoors or out, or for porch picnic.

MENU

CALIFORNIA HAM CASSEROLE
SMALL CURRANT-JELLY SANDWICHES
CARROT STICKS RADISHES
DATE-PECAN ICE CREAM SOFT GINGER COOKIES
COFFEE

DEVILED HAM SLICES

4 slices baked ham (¼-inch)
2 tablespoons brown sugar
1 teaspoon cornstarch
⅛ teaspoon each: salt, cinnamon, cloves
½ teaspoon A.1. sauce
½ cup Chablis or dry sherry
1 tablespoon vinegar
¼ cup seedless raisins or currants
1 tablespoon butter or margarine

Place ham slices, slightly overlapping, in small baking dish. Combine remaining ingredients; cook over low heat stirring constantly until well mixed and hot. Let boil one minute. Pour over ham. Bake in moderate oven (375° F.) about twenty-five minutes. Baste every five minutes until ham is glazed and hot. 4 servings.

Just right for TV supper with brown-and-serve rolls and coffee.

MENU

CHABLIS OR SHERRY — PÂTÉ DE FOIE GRAS
BUTTERED THIN TOAST
DEVILED HAM SLICES
BUTTERED SPINACH
PINEAPPLE SHERBET — MERINGUE COOKIES
COFFEE

EASY HAM PIE

1½ cups cubed cooked ham
1 cup cooked quick-frozen peas-and-carrots
1 cup cubed boiled potatoes
1½ cups medium white sauce
2 tablespoons chopped parsley
2 tablespoons chopped canned mushrooms
Cheese biscuit-mix for 6 biscuits
1 tablespoon grated Parmesan cheese

Arrange layers of ham, vegetables, and white sauce in a greased casserole (two-quart). Sprinkle white sauce layers with parsley and mushrooms. Mix biscuits as described on package; cut in rounds and place on top of casserole mixture. Sprinkle biscuits lightly with grated cheese. Bake in hot oven (425° F.) thirty minutes, or until biscuits are risen and lightly browned. Serve hot. 6 servings.

For Easy Chicken Pie, Easy Turkey Pie, Easy Veal Pie, *follow same recipe.*

MENU

COCKTAILS
SARDINE-AND-CREAM-CHEESE DIP
CELERY CRACKERS
EASY HAM PIE
TOMATO ASPIC HORSE-RADISH MAYONNAISE
BRANDIED PEACHES
COFFEE

OVEN JAMBALAYA

1 tablespoon butter or margarine
1 tablespoon flour
1 pound ham, cut in slender sticks
1 cup cooked, canned, or quick-frozen shrimp
1½ cups canned tomatoes
1 onion, peeled and chopped
1 green pepper, chopped
1 clove garlic, peeled, halved
1 teaspoon each: salt, Worcestershire sauce, thyme
¼ teaspoon Tabasco sauce
½ teaspoon paprika
4 cups water
1 cup rice

Melt butter in a flameproof casserole (two-quart); stir flour in smoothly; add ham, cleaned shrimp, tomatoes; stir and cook seven minutes. Add onion, green pepper, garlic, seasonings, and water. Let come to boiling; boil ten minutes. Add rice. Cover dish; place in moderate oven (350° F.) and cook twenty minutes, or until rice is done. Do not stir. Lift mixture with fork a few times to prevent rice burning. 6 servings.

A New Orleans specialty, hearty and well-flavored.

MENU

OVEN JAMBALAYA
BAKED MACARONI AND CHEESE
BOSTON BROWN-BREAD FINGER SANDWICHES
COLESLAW WITH APPLE AND CELERY   MAYONNAISE
COFFEE JELLY   NUT POUNDCAKE
COFFEE   LIQUEURS

HASH WITH CHEESE TOPPING

1½ cups corned beef hash
3 tablespoons prepared mustard
1 tablespoon prepared horse-radish
6 slices bread
3 tablespoons chopped ripe olives
3 tablespoons chopped peeled onion
6 thin slices Tilsit, Muenster, or Swiss cheese

Combine hash with mustard and horse-radish; spread bread. Place slices in wide, shallow metal-base baking dish. Sprinkle with olives and onion. Lay cheese on top. Bake in hot oven (425° F.) ten minutes, or until cheese is melted and brown. 6 servings.

Serve ale, beer, or other favorite beverage with this specialty.

MENU

HASH WITH CHEESE TOPPING
HOT MINCEMEAT TARTS
COFFEE

MACARONI-AND-HAM SOUFFLÉ

1 package (8-ounce) ziti or elbow macaroni
1 cup ground cooked ham
2 cups grated mild cheese
2 tablespoons chopped peeled onion
1 sweet red pepper, chopped fine
1 green pepper, chopped fine
½ teaspoon salt
¼ teaspoon dry mustard
⅛ teaspoon nutmeg
4 eggs

Cook macaroni as described on package; drain. Add ham, and all but two tablespoons of the cheese. Add onion, peppers, and seasonings. Beat yolks until light, and combine with macaroni mixture. Whip egg whites stiff and fold in. Pour into greased casserole (two-quart). Sprinkle top with remaining two tablespoons of cheese. Set dish in shallow pan of hot water. Bake in moderate oven (350° F.) thirty to forty minutes, until risen and lightly browned. Serve at once. 8 servings.

For Macaroni-and-Tuna Soufflé, Macaroni-and-Chicken Soufflé, *follow same recipe.*

MENU

MACARONI-AND-HAM SOUFFLÉ
TOMATO CHUTNEY PICKLE RELISH
TINY WHOLE-WHEAT BISCUITS
PECAN PIE
COFFEE

BOWKNOTS WITH VEGETABLES

(MARY GIBBONS, NEW YORK)

- 1 package (8-ounce) Buitoni egg-pasta bowknots
- 2 cups cubed cooked white meat chicken
- 1 cup canned or cooked mushrooms
- 6 small cooked white onions
- 3 cooked carrots, diced
- 1 tablespoon butter or chicken fat
- 1 teaspoon flour
- 2 cups light cream, top milk, or chicken stock
- 3 eggs
- 1 teaspoon salt
- ½ teaspoon pepper
- ½ teaspoon grated lemon peel
- ¼ cup chopped or slivered almonds
- 1 teaspoon dried celery leaves
- 1 tablespoon chopped parsley
- 1 cup Melba toast crumbs

Cook bowknots in boiling salted water fifteen minutes, or until almost tender. Drain; plunge into cold water; drain on folded towel. Pour into buttered oblong casserole (two-quart). Add chicken; then layers of mushrooms, onions, and carrots. Melt butter or chicken fat in saucepan; stir flour smoothly in; add cream, milk, or stock, stirring and cooking ten minutes, or until thickened. Remove from heat. Beat eggs until creamy; add with salt, pepper, peel, almonds, celery leaves, and parsley. Pour over mixture in casserole. Top with crumbs. Set in shallow pan of hot water. Bake in moderate oven (350° F.) thirty minutes, or until browned. 6 servings.

A delicious macaroni dish for buffet or as dinner main dish.

MENU

COCKTAILS SHARP CHEESE SPREAD
BOWKNOTS WITH VEGETABLES
CRANBERRY JELLY BROWN-AND-SERVE FRENCH BREAD
STRAWBERRIES WITH KIRSCH COFFEE

ITALIAN MEAT BALLS WITH SPAGHETTI

1 package (8-ounce) spaghetti
3 slices bread
1 pound ground beef
3 eggs
3 tablespoons grated Romano cheese
1 clove garlic, peeled and chopped
2 tablespoons chopped parsley
1 teaspoon salt
½ teaspoon pepper
Flour
6 tablespoons olive oil
3 tablespoons grated Parmesan cheese
Paprika

Cook spaghetti as described on package. Drain. Soak bread in one-half cup water five minutes; squeeze dry. Mix with beef, beaten eggs, Romano cheese, garlic, and parsley. Add salt and pepper. Shape into two-inch balls. Roll in flour; sauté in hot oil in shallow (metal-base) flameproof baking dish ten minutes, or until browned. Add spaghetti to dish. Spoon some of the oil in the dish over the spaghetti. Sprinkle top with Parmesan and lightly with paprika. Bake fifteen minutes in hot oven (425° F.). 4 to 6 servings.

Makes fine one-dish meal with Chianti or B&G Sparkling Burgundy.

MENU

TOMATO JUICE
WATER-CRESS AND ANCHOVY CANAPÉS
ITALIAN MEAT BALLS WITH SPAGHETTI
CHIANTI OR BURGUNDY
MELON SLICES COFFEE

NOODLES WITH VEAL

1½ pounds veal, cubed
Salt and pepper
½ bay leaf
1 package (8-ounce) noodles
1 can (10½-ounce) condensed chicken soup
1 green pepper, chopped
1 pimiento, chopped
2 tablespoons chopped canned mushrooms
¼ cup buttered bread crumbs
3 tablespoons grated mild cheese

Cover veal with water; add light seasoning of salt and pepper, and bay leaf. Bring to boiling; lower heat and let boil gently forty minutes, or until tender. Cook noodles, as described on package; drain. Combine drained veal, noodles, soup, green pepper, pimiento, and mushrooms. Pour into buttered casserole (two-quart). If too dry add a little stock in which the veal cooked. Cover with crumbs and cheese. Bake in moderate oven (350° F.) thirty minutes, or until bubbly and browned. 6 to 8 servings.

Salad and dessert may be omitted; a one-dish meal for family and guests.

MENU

COCKTAILS TINY CODFISH BALLS
PAPRIKA CRACKERS
NOODLES WITH VEAL
TOSSED GREEN SALAD
RED PLUM TART COFFEE

FRIDAY NIGHT OYSTERS

12 large oysters, shelled, or
 quick-frozen oysters, defrosted
2 tablespoons butter or margarine
1 tablespoon chopped parsley
¼ teaspoon pepper
½ teaspoon salt
½ cup Chablis or other dry white wine
1 tablespoon flour
2 tablespoons heavy cream
¼ cup buttered cracker crumbs
Paprika

Heat oysters in their liquor in saucepan with one tablespoon butter or margarine, the parsley, pepper, salt, and wine. Heat until steaming; remove from heat before boiling begins. Drain oysters, saving liquid. Place oysters in buttered shallow baking dish (one and one-half quart). Reduce sauce a little by boiling; stir remaining tablespoon of butter and the flour smoothly together; stir into sauce; add cream; stir and cook until slightly thickened. Pour over oysters in dish. Sprinkle with crumbs and paprika. Bake in moderate oven (375° F.) fifteen minutes. Serve hot. 4 servings.

Appetizing as first course when baked in scallop shells.

MENU

SHERRY MIXED CANAPÉS
FRIDAY NIGHT OYSTERS
BROWN-AND-SERVE RYE ROLLS
VEGETABLE SALAD
(SCALLIONS, CUCUMBERS, COOKED GREEN BEANS AND SLICED TOMATOES)
FRENCH DRESSING
COFFEE

EASY PIZZA

Biscuit-mix
1 can (17-ounce) tomatoes
Salt and pepper
1 cup cubed sharp cheese
1 cup cubed chopped salami or Vienna sausage
2 tablespoons olive oil
1 teaspoon orégano
½ teaspoon basil
1 tablespoon chopped parsley
1 tablespoon chopped chives

Prepare dough according to package directions. Roll thin; shape to fit bottom and sides of a greased nine-inch baking dish. Drain tomatoes; chop; pour over pastry. Sprinkle lightly with salt and pepper. Dot with cheese and sausage or salami. Spoon oil lightly over all. Sprinkle with herbs, parsley, and chives. Bake in hot oven (450° F.) twenty minutes, or until pastry is browned. 6 servings.

Vary this by using chopped anchovies in place of sausage.

MENU

EASY PIZZA
WARM DEEP-DISH APPLE PIE
ALE BEER COFFEE

PIZZA FOR EIGHT

Rich pie pastry, or pastry-mix
Olive oil
3 cans (6-ounce) tomato paste
⅓ cup water
1 pound sausage meat, cooked
1 clove garlic, peeled and chopped fine
½ cup grated Parmesan cheese
1 teaspoon orégano
½ teaspoon salt
1 cup chopped olives
½ cup chopped anchovy fillets
2 cups grated sharp cheese

Mix pastry; roll out in two pieces to fit bottom of greased, large, shallow, oblong baking dishes. (Metal-base flameproof type of baker.) Brush dough with olive oil. Combine tomato paste with just enough water to spread over dough. Add sausage and garlic to each dish. Sprinkle with Parmesan, orégano, and salt. Add olives and anchovies. Top with cheese. Bake in hot oven (425° F.) thirty minutes. Cut at buffet table while hot. Each baking dish makes four large servings eaten out of hand. 8 servings.

Richer corn-meal-and-flour pastry is more authentically Italian.

MENU

PIZZA FOR EIGHT
FRUIT BOWL OF APPLES,
PEARS, GRAPES, PLUMS
COFFEE

MUSHROOM SCALLOPED POTATOES

8 medium-sized potatoes, pared and sliced
½ cup chopped green pepper
½ cup chopped peeled onions
1 can (3-ounce) sliced broiled mushrooms
1 tablespoon salt
½ teaspoon white pepper
1 can (10½-ounce) condensed cream of mushroom soup
1 cup milk (about)

Make alternate layers of potatoes, green pepper, onions, and mushrooms in a greased baking dish (two-quart). Season layers lightly. Mix mushroom soup and milk, and pour over all. Liquid should show in top layer; add more if needed. Cover; bake in moderate oven (350° F.) one hour and fifteen minutes. Uncover dish and continue baking fifteen minutes to brown top. 6 to 8 servings.

Good at brunch, or on a picnic, or as part of larger menu.

MENU

SHERRY TOASTED CHEESE CANAPÉS OLIVES
MUSHROOM SCALLOPED POTATOES
BOLOGNA CERVELAT COLD TONGUE
BUTTERED BROWN BREAD
BLACK CHERRY AND ALMOND GELATIN
CUSTARD SAUCE *
COFFEE

HEARTY RICE CASSEROLE

(MARION CLYDE MCCARROLL, NEW YORK)

1⅓ cups Minute rice
2½ cups milk
¾ teaspoon salt
2 cups grated sharp cheese
⅛ teaspoon each: freshly-ground pepper, dry mustard,
  Worcestershire sauce
1 cup quick-frozen mixed vegetables, defrosted
½ cup soft bread crumbs

Combine rice, milk, and salt in saucepan; mix just enough to moisten all rice. Bring quickly to boiling. Cover; lower heat and let simmer three minutes. Add cheese, pepper, mustard, and Worcestershire. Mix well. Stir vegetables in. Pour into buttered baking dish (one-quart). Sprinkle with crumbs. Bake in moderate oven (350° F.) fifteen minutes, or until browned. 4 to 6 servings.

A good television supper dish with salad and coffee.

MENU

CANTALOUPE BALLS WITH ORANGE JUICE
HEARTY RICE CASSEROLE
SLICED MEAT LOAF   LIVERWURST   HAM
ASSORTED BREADS   MUSTARD PICKLE
LEMON SHERBET   PECAN COOKIES
COFFEE

WILD RICE AND CHICKEN LIVERS

(JEANNE AND HOWARD SMITH, LANSDOWNE, PENNSYLVANIA)

1 cup wild rice
3 cups boiling water
½ teaspoon Better Products all-purpose seasoning
⅛ teaspoon thyme
6 sprigs parsley
2 sprigs celery leaves
½ bay leaf
1 medium-sized onion, peeled and chopped
7 tablespoons butter or margarine
1 pound chicken livers, cut in pieces

Wash rice under running water until water runs clear. Drain; cover with cold water and let soak thirty minutes. Drain; cover with boiling water in saucepan; add seasoning, thyme, parsley, celery and bay leaves. Cover; bring to boiling, lower heat, simmer gently forty-five minutes, or until rice is tender. Stir frequently; add more water if necessary. Sauté onion in four tablespoons butter or margarine until golden. Add chicken livers, and cook five minutes. Combine livers and cooked rice, and any liquid remaining in rice; discard parsley and celery leaves. Pour into buttered casserole (one-quart). Dot top with remaining three tablespoons butter or margarine. Bake in moderate oven (375° F.) fifteen minutes. 4 to 6 servings.

Hearty enough to serve as a one-dish meal with favorite beverage.

MENU

BAKED TONGUE SPICED PEARS
WILD RICE AND CHICKEN LIVERS HOT ROLLS
APPLES PEARS
EDAM AND PORT DU SALUT CHEESE
COFFEE

BAKED SARDINES

2 tablespoons butter or margarine
¼ cup Chablis or other dry white wine
½ teaspoon anchovy paste
Juice ½ lemon
12 large boneless sardines
Salt
Mace
Cayenne
¼ cup buttered bread crumbs

Melt butter or margarine in a shallow flameproof baking dish. Add wine, anchovy paste, and lemon juice. Stir to mix. Remove from heat. Arrange sardines in the dish. Season lightly with salt, mace, and cayenne. Cover with buttered crumbs. Bake in moderately-hot oven (400° F.) until top is browned. 4 servings.

A good quickie for unexpected guests or bridge supper.

MENU

COLD VICHYSSOISE
BAKED SARDINES SCALLOPED TOMATOES
CHABLIS
LARGE ITALIAN WHOLE-WHEAT LOAF
TO SLICE AT TABLE
GUAVA JELLY CREAM CHEESE
COFFEE

IRISH SAUSAGE SUPPER

1 pound pork sausage
2 apples, pared and sliced
2 onions, peeled and sliced
1 tablespoon flour
Salt and pepper
1 cup stock or bouillon
2 to 3 cups hot mashed potatoes

Fry sausages slowly until golden brown. Drain; place in nine-inch baking dish. Cook apples and onions in sausage fat ten minutes. Spoon over sausages. Pour off all but one tablespoon of fat. Brown flour in fat left in pan. Add seasonings and stock or bouillon. Stir until thickened. Pour over sausages. Top with mashed potatoes. Bake in moderate oven (350° F.) fifteen minutes, or until potatoes are golden. 4 or 5 servings.

You don't have to be Irish to enjoy this one. And try it for brunch.

MENU

COCKTAILS
SMOKED SALMON CANAPÉS
IRISH SAUSAGE SUPPER
HOT CORN BREAD GRAPE BUTTER
CARAMEL CUSTARD
COFFEE

SEA-FOOD MÉLANGE

(WILMA FREEMAN, NEW YORK)

8 tablespoons butter
½ teaspoon white pepper
½ teaspoon salt
¼ teaspoon dry mustard
¼ cup chopped peeled onion
¼ cup chopped green pepper
½ pound (1 cup) cooked, canned, or
  quick-frozen crab meat (defrosted)
½ pound (1 cup) cooked, canned, or
  quick-frozen lobster (defrosted)
¼ cup Rhine wine

Melt butter in heavy saucepan or skillet; add seasonings, onions, and green pepper. Cook, and stir five minutes, or until onions and pepper are tender. Add sea food, and stir to coat well with the sauce. Turn mixture into a buttered baking dish (one-quart). Bake in preheated moderate oven (350° F.) fifteen minutes. Turn heat off; add wine to dish, stir; cover casserole. Close oven door and let dish stay ten minutes. Serve on toast points, crackers, or split and toasted rolls. 4 or 5 servings.

Rich, delicious. For special-occasion supper guests.

MENU

SEA-FOOD MÉLANGE   TOAST POINTS
ASPARAGUS, TOMATO, WATER-CRESS SALAD
FRENCH DRESSING
LIME SHERBET ON SLICED STRAWBERRIES
COFFEE

SAVORY BAKED SHRIMP

1½ pounds cooked, canned, or quick-frozen shrimp (defrosted)
¼ teaspoon mace
½ teaspoon pepper
2 cups medium white sauce
¼ cup chili sauce
¼ teaspoon dry mustard
¼ cup sherry or dry white wine
¼ cup buttered crumbs
Paprika

Clean shrimp of dark vein; rinse. Add seasonings to white sauce; blend in chili sauce, mustard, wine, and shrimp. Pour into buttered casserole (one and one-half quart) and cover with crumbs. Sprinkle lightly with paprika. Bake in moderately-hot oven (400° F.) until bubbly and browning. 6 servings.

For Savory Baked Scallops *substitute cooked small scallops.*

MENU

HOT TOMATO BOUILLON
STUFFED CELERY HEARTS
SAVORY BAKED SHRIMP
CABBAGE, ONION, AND GREEN PEPPER SALAD
FRENCH DRESSING
CHEESE CAKE
COFFEE

SHRIMP ON RICE

(SUE PROSSER, NEW YORK)

2 cups cooked, canned, or quick-frozen shrimp (defrosted)
2 cups light cream
2 cups cooked rice
1 tablespoon butter or margarine
3/8 cup catsup
6 drops Tabasco sauce
1 tablespoon Worcestershire sauce
Salt, if needed

Remove dark vein from shrimp; rinse and drain. Combine all ingredients in a buttered casserole (one and one-half quart). Bake, covered, in moderate oven (350° F.) thirty-five minutes; uncover, and bake five minutes longer. Serve hot with chutney. 4 servings.

Quick and easy using quick-frozen shrimp and Minute rice.

MENU

MADEIRA OR DRY SHERRY
DEVILED EGG APPETIZER
SHRIMP ON RICE
SMALL BROWN-AND-SERVE BISCUITS
CHUTNEY APPLE JELLY
FRESH PINEAPPLE SLICES
COFFEE

BUFFET CELERY SOUP

3 cans (10½-ounce) condensed celery soup
1 quart milk
1 cup light cream
½ teaspoon celery salt
Black pepper
1 cup heavy cream, whipped
2 tablespoons chopped celery tops
2 tablespoons cut chives
Parmesan cheese

Combine soup, milk, light cream, and celery salt in large kettle. Stir and heat just to boiling point. Pour at once into warmed soup casserole, place over low heat on buffet table. Add light grinding of black pepper to top of soup. Cover, and let stand. Combine whipped cream with celery tops and chives. Add spoonful to each soup bowl before serving soup. Sprinkle filled bowls with cheese. Or pour the soup into individual casseroles; top each with spoonful of whipped-cream mixture; sprinkle with cheese. Place casseroles in a moderate oven (375° F.) ten minutes. 6 servings.

When cheese is omitted, a little curry powder makes a flavorful addition.

MENU

BUFFET CELERY SOUP
CRUSTY FRENCH BREAD WITH HERB BUTTER
FLAMING BRANDIED PEACHES
AND CHERRIES IN A CHAFING DISH
POUNDCAKE COFFEE

COUNTRY GARDEN SOUP

6 scallions
¼ pound mushrooms
6 cups mixed raw vegetables
(1 cup each: Lima beans, peas, cut green beans, chopped celery, sliced carrots, cauliflower)
5 cups boiling water
1 tablespoon salt
2 cups bouillon
½ cup heavy cream or sour cream
¼ cup chopped fresh parsley
2 tablespoons chopped scallion tops
1 tablespoon orégano
½ cup heavy cream, whipped stiff
Freshly-ground pepper

Chop or slice white part of scallions (save the tops). Stem, peel, and slice mushrooms. Combine vegetables and mushrooms in a three-quart kettle; pour in boiling water, add salt. Cover, and boil gently until vegetables are tender, twenty-five to thirty minutes. Add the bouillon; stir, and add cream or sour cream. Mix; let boil gently five minutes. Combine parsley, scallion tops, and orégano with whipped cream in a warmed soup casserole. Add hot soup. Guests grind pepper on their servings if desired. 8 servings.

For a change, use chopped spinach or lettuce in place of green beans.

MENU

COCKTAILS CRISP POTATO STICKS
COUNTRY GARDEN SOUP
COLD CUTS AND CHEESE
WHOLE-WHEAT ITALIAN BREAD
MOCHA SOUFFLÉ * COFFEE

HALIBUT OVEN CHOWDER

2 pounds fresh or quick-frozen fillets of halibut
2 sprigs parsley
½ bay leaf
6 medium-sized potatoes, pared and sliced thin
4 leeks, sliced thin
1½ tablespoons salt
¼ teaspoon black pepper
16 squares saltines, or 4 sea toast crackers, crumbled
4 cups milk
½ cup light cream
1 tablespoon Worcestershire sauce
Paprika
2 tablespoons chopped chives

If frozen fillets are used, defrost. Cut fish in small pieces; combine with parsley, bay leaf, and four cups water in a two-quart kettle. Bring to boiling, lower heat, cover, and simmer twenty minutes. Drain fish, saving the stock. Arrange half of the fish in the bottom of a three- or four-quart soup casserole. Cover with half the potatoes and leeks; season; cover with crackers. Repeat layers; season top; cover with crackers. Combine strained fish stock and milk and pour over top. Cover; bake in moderate oven (375° F.) forty-five minutes. Uncover; stir cream in; let cook fifteen minutes. Stir in Worcestershire. Remove casserole to table; sprinkle top lightly with paprika and chives. 8 servings.

Makes a fine Lenten supper with cheese, fruit, and coffee.

MENU

HALIBUT OVEN CHOWDER
BUTTERED AND HEATED SEA TOAST CRACKERS
FRESH PEARS AND SEEDLESS GRAPES
EDAM CHEESE   COFFEE

HERB GREEN-TURTLE SOUP

½ teaspoon each: crumbled dried leaf sage,
 parsley, marjoram, rosemary,
 thyme, sweet basil, and mint leaves
½ bay leaf
4 allspice berries
2 coriander seeds, crushed
1/16 teaspoon anise seeds
4 whole cloves
2 cans (13-ounce) green-turtle soup
3 cans (10½-ounce) condensed cream of pea soup
2 cans (10½-ounce) bouillon
Salt and pepper

Crumble dried herbs together with bay leaf; combine with allspice, coriander, anise, and cloves. Add to turtle soup in a saucepan and heat about five minutes, or until soup just reaches boiling point. Strain the soup and save the herb mixture. Combine strained turtle soup with pea soup and bouillon in a large warmed soup casserole. Add salt and pepper if needed. Place on warmer on buffet table to heat thoroughly. Divide soup-herbs into eight portions; add to soup cups or bowls. Ladle hot soup into the bowls and serve. 8 servings.

This is a super soup. Serve as main dish or with soufflé.

MENU

HERB GREEN-TURTLE SOUP
CRUSTY FRENCH ROLLS
EASY HAM SOUFFLÉ *
RHINE WINE
CHOCOLATE LEAF COOKIES MADELEINES
COFFEE

OYSTER SAM'S STEW

2 dozen oysters, or
    2 packages (12-ounce) quick-frozen oysters
1 cup oyster liquor
1 cup sliced celery
3 tablespoons butter
1 tablespoon chopped celery tops
3 cups milk
1 cup light cream
2 teaspoons salt
½ teaspoon black pepper
2 teaspoons Worcestershire sauce
Paprika
Pilot or sea toast crackers

If frozen oysters are used, defrost as described on package. Drain oysters. Combine liquor, celery, and two tablespoons of butter in a large saucepan. Cover, and boil gently fifteen minutes. Remove from heat; add celery tops; cover, and let stand a few minutes. Scald milk and cream together; add salt, pepper, and Worcestershire. Add oysters to liquor and celery; cook about four minutes, until oysters are plump and edges rippled. Add hot milk and cream, and remaining tablespoon of butter. Heat only long enough for the butter to melt. Pour into warmed soup casserole; sprinkle top with paprika. Set casserole over warmer on table. Serve with crackers broken into the bowls. 8 servings.

And just as good at brunch on a cold Sunday morning.

MENU

OYSTER SAM'S STEW
JELLIED GRAPEFRUIT SALAD
(APPLE, CANNED PINEAPPLE, CHERRIES)
ORANGE FRENCH DRESSING
ASSORTED ICED CUPCAKES   COFFEE

SPAGHETTI AND LIVER CASSEROLE

1-pound slice liver (beef or calf)
2 tablespoons flour
3 tablespoons fat
½ cup chopped peeled onions
1½ teaspoons Kitchen Bouquet
3½ cups (29-ounce can) canned tomatoes
1½ teaspoons salt
1 teaspoon sugar
⅛ teaspoon each: orégano, pepper, mace
1 tablespoon chopped parsley
1 can (3-ounce) sliced broiled mushrooms
1 package (8-ounce) spaghetti
Grated Parmesan cheese

Cover liver with boiling water and let stand five minutes. Drain well and blot with paper toweling. Remove any tubing and skin. Cut liver in narrow strips. Sprinkle evenly with flour. Melt fat in large frying pan over moderate heat. Add liver and brown lightly on both sides. Add onions and let cook five minutes longer. Stir in Kitchen Bouquet. Add tomatoes, seasonings, parsley, mushrooms, and their liquid. Bring to boiling, lower heat, and simmer fifteen minutes. Cook spaghetti as described on package, until barely tender. Drain; combine with liver sauce. Pour into baking dish (two-quart); brown in moderate oven (350° F.) fifteen minutes. Serve topped with grated Parmesan cheese. 4 or 5 servings.

Chopped chicken livers and giblets may be substituted for beef liver.

MENU

DRIED BEEF AND CUCUMBER CANAPÉS — COCKTAILS
SPAGHETTI AND LIVER CASSEROLE — HOT GRAHAM ROLLS
BLUEBERRY PIE — COFFEE

APPLE-STUFFED ACORN SQUASH

2 acorn squash
3 tart red apples
1 cup broken cashew nuts
½ cup maple sirup
¼ cup melted butter or margarine
Extra butter

Wash squash; cut in half lengthwise. Scoop out seeds and stringy substance. Wash, core, and dice unpared apples. Combine with remaining ingredients. Fill squash halves with apple mixture. Brush squash surfaces with additional butter or margarine. Set in baking dish. Pour hot water in to depth of one-half inch. Cover dish, Bake in moderately-hot oven (400° F.) forty-five minutes. Uncover for last five minutes of baking. 4 servings.

Good autumn flavor in this. Serve as main dish or with roast.

MENU

CRANBERRY JUICE
CHEESE CRACKERS
BAKED HAM SLICE
MUSTARD PICKLE RED PEPPER RELISH
APPLE-STUFFED ACORN SQUASH
BROWN-AND-SERVE RAISIN ROLLS BUTTER
MINCEMEAT PIE
COFFEE

OVEN SUKIYAKI

1 pound round steak
½ pound mushrooms
1 Bermuda onion, peeled
3 stalks celery
1 can (8-ounce) bamboo shoots
Beef suet
3 tablespoons sugar
⅓ cup soy (shoyu) sauce
1 tablespoon saki or sherry
½ cup bouillon
2 cups (½ pound) spinach leaves

Slice steak very thin diagonally across the grain. Wash vegetables; drain; slice very thin. Drain bamboo shoots and slice. Use piece of beef suet to grease (metal-base) flameproof baking dish. Brown beef quickly; add all ingredients except spinach. Cover; place in hot oven (425° F.) and cook twenty minutes, stirring frequently. Add washed spinach; cook ten minutes longer. To American taste vegetables seem semi-cooked. Serve hot with hot rice. 4 servings.

Pretty Japanese wares make a gala occasion with this dish.

MENU

HOT BOUILLON WITH SLICED LEEKS
OVEN SUKIYAKI
HOT RICE
SLICED PICKLES CUCUMBER STICKS
PRESERVED KUMQUATS AND APRICOTS
ALMOND COOKIES
TEA OR COFFEE

SWEETBREADS AND HAM CASSEROLE

2 pounds sweetbreads
Juice 1 lemon
⅓ cup butter or margarine
⅓ cup flour
1½ cups canned chicken broth
1 cup light cream
¼ teaspoon salt
½ teaspoon paprika
½ teaspoon onion salt
¼ teaspoon celery salt
1 teaspoon Worcestershire sauce
1½ cups cubed cooked ham
½ cup sliced toasted almonds
8 small triangles toast

Soak sweetbreads in cold water one hour; drain. Cover with two quarts water, add lemon juice, and bring to boiling. Reduce heat; simmer twenty minutes. Drain; remove membrane; dice sweetbreads. Melt butter or margarine; stir flour in smoothly; gradually stir in chicken broth and cream; cook and stir constantly until thick. Add sweetbreads and remaining ingredients except toast. Pour into greased casserole (two-quart). Top with toast triangles. Bake in hot oven (425° F.) ten minutes, until top is bubbly. 6 to 8 servings.

Rich; intended for gala party. Luncheon favorite, too.

MENU

SWEETBREADS AND HAM CASSEROLE
EXTRA TOAST TRIANGLES
OLIVES SWEET PICKLES WATERMELON PICKLE
RASPBERRY SHERBET ASSORTED COOKIES
COFFEE

DALLAS TAMALE PIE

(HELEN AND CHARLES HOVEY, NEW YORK)

1 can (20-ounce) cream-style corn
1 can (20-ounce) tomatoes
1½ cups yellow corn meal
½ cup shortening
1 medium-sized onion, peeled and chopped
2 cloves garlic, peeled and chopped
1 green pepper, chopped
1 pound ground beef
Salt and pepper
1½ tablespoons chili powder
½ cup chopped ripe olives

Heat corn and tomatoes together in a two-quart saucepan. When boiling, stir in corn meal. Cook, stirring constantly two minutes, or until thick. Remove from heat. Melt shortening in a flameproof baking dish (two-quart). Sauté onion, garlic, and green pepper eight minutes, or until onion is golden. Add beef, stir and season with salt, pepper, and chili powder. Add olives. Mix, and cook five minutes. Blend in the corn-and-tomato mixture. Bake in moderately-low oven (300° F.) one and one-half hours. 8 servings.

Hot fare for strong men and hungry girls.

MENU

COCKTAILS   POTATO CHIPS
AVOCADO DIP
DALLAS TAMALE PIE
GRAPEFRUIT, APPLE, PRUNE SALAD
SOUR CREAM DRESSING
COFFEE

MEXICAN TAMALE CASSEROLE

3 tablespoons fat
¼ cup chopped peeled onions
2 cloves garlic, peeled and chopped
2 cups chopped cooked beef
½ cup chopped ripe olives
1 cup canned tomatoes
½ cup meat stock or bouillon
1 tablespoon chili powder
3 teaspoons salt
2 cups yellow corn meal
5 cups boiling water

Melt two tablespoons of fat in a heavy frying pan. Brown onions and garlic. Add beef, olives, tomatoes, stock or bouillon, chili powder, and one teaspoon salt. Stir; simmer slowly twenty minutes. Prepare mush by stirring the corn meal and remaining two teaspoons salt into the water. Add remaining tablespoon of fat. Cook very slowly, stirring frequently, for fifteen minutes. Do not cook until dry. Line bottom and sides of greased casserole (two-quart) with mush, reserving some for top. Pour simmered meat mixture into mush-lined casserole; top with remaining mush. Bake in moderate oven (350° F.) forty-five minutes. 4 to 6 servings.

When raw beef is used, cook with onion, garlic, and additional fat until almost done, about twenty-five minutes. Then follow recipe.

A favorite with teen-agers. Use Mexican trays and casserole.

MENU

MEXICAN TAMALE CASSEROLE
INDIVIDUAL LEMON-FRUIT GELATIN SALADS
(GRAPES, BLACK CHERRIES, AND ORANGE)
ORANGE FRENCH DRESSING
FUDGE-FROSTED SPICE CAKE COFFEE

WESTERN GANG SUPPER

1 cup ripe olives
1 can (15- or 16-ounce) tamales
1 pound ground beef
1 tablespoon oil
1 medium-sized onion, peeled and chopped
1 can (8-ounce) tomato sauce
1 can (10½-ounce) consommé
1 can (12-ounce) whole kernel corn
1 teaspoon salt
2 teaspoons chili powder
2 packages (3½-ounce) corn chips
½ cup grated American cheese

Cut olives in large pieces. Drain tamales, reserving liquid; cut in half-inch slices. Grease a baking dish (two-quart) and line with tamale slices. Brown beef in oil. Add onion and brown lightly. Add olives and all remaining ingredients except cheese. Heat to boiling. Turn into lined baking dish; top with cheese. Bake in moderate oven (350° F.) thirty to forty-five minutes. 8 to 10 servings.

Flavorful and good for porch picnic, too.

MENU

WESTERN GANG SUPPER
SMALL ROLLS, TOASTED AND BUTTERED
SPICED CRAB APPLES   PICKLE RELISH
HOT APRICOT TURNOVERS WITH VANILLA ICE CREAM
COFFEE   COLD DRINKS

BEEF TONGUE WITH ANCHOVIES

4- to 5-pound boiled beef tongue
10 anchovy fillets
¼ pound butter
4 tablespoons chopped parsley
¼ cup melted butter or margarine
1 teaspoon prepared mustard

Skin and trim tongue. Cut in slices, but do not cut entirely through. Mash fillets with butter, and blend thoroughly. Spread tongue slices generously with anchovy butter. Sprinkle with parsley. Reshape tongue; place in shallow (metal-base) baking dish. Pour melted butter or margarine mixed with mustard over it. Bake in moderate oven (350° F.) thirty minutes. Serve hot. 8 servings.

Extra good when three tablespoons coarse crumbs are stirred into butter-mustard mixture.

MENU

COCKTAILS
SMOKED CHEESE PICKLED ONIONS
ASSORTED CRACKERS
BEEF TONGUE WITH ANCHOVIES
BROWN RICE WITH ALMONDS
HOT FRUIT COMPOTE WITH KIRSCH
(BLACK CHERRIES, SLICED CLING PEACHES)
COFFEE

SPICED TURKISH TONGUES

12 lamb's tongues
1 teaspoon salt
6 whole cloves
2 little red-pepper pods
1 bay leaf
1 medium-sized onion, peeled and sliced
2 large carrots
1½ cups seedless raisins
1 cup fresh California dates
8 walnut halves
2 tablespoons butter or margarine
2 tablespoons flour
1 cup broth

Wash tongues. Drain. Add salt, cloves, pepper pods, bay leaf, onion, and water to cover. Simmer, covered, two hours. Let stand in broth until cool enough to handle. Drain, saving broth. Remove skin, bones, and fat from tongues. Place in large casserole. Wash carrots; scrape and slice. Wash and drain raisins. Pit and cut up dates. Arrange around tongues. Add walnuts. Melt butter, stir in flour and one cup of broth the tongues were cooked in. Cook until smooth and thick, stirring constantly. Pour sauce over tongues. Cover and bake in moderate oven (375° F.) one and one-half hours. The sauce becomes rich and dark and is absorbed by the meat. 8 to 10 servings.

Unusually good flavor for family and guest enjoyment.

MENU

COCKTAILS ROLLED TOASTED CHEESE CANAPÉS
SPICED TURKISH TONGUES HOT RICE OR WHEAT PILAF
CHABLIS
WINE JELLY ASSORTED SMALL CUPCAKES COFFEE

casseroles ar

easy on the budget

LIMA BEANS WITH TOMATO SAUCE

1 cup dried Lima beans, or
3 cups cooked Limas
¼ pound fat bacon or ham, diced
½ cup chopped peeled onions
1 cup canned tomato sauce
2 tablespoons chopped parsley
½ teaspoon salt
⅛ teaspoon celery salt
⅛ teaspoon cayenne
½ teaspoon orégano

Wash dried Lima beans, drain, cover with cold water and let soak overnight. Drain, cover with one quart cold water and boil one and one-half to two hours, or until beans are tender. Drain. Cook bacon or ham in frying pan five minutes; add onions, and cook five minutes. Add cooked Limas, mix well, and pour into a baking dish (one and one-half quart). Combine tomato sauce, parsley, salt, celery salt, and cayenne. Pour over beans. Cover casserole; cook in moderate oven (350° F.) one and one-half hours. Uncover dish, stir orégano in and bake another half hour. Beans should be very tender; if not, continue baking. 6 servings.

Crusty crumb topping is liked by some on this casserole.

MENU

CANTALOUPE WITH FRESH LEMON
LIMA BEANS WITH TOMATO SAUCE
TOASTED SPLIT ENGLISH MUFFINS   APRICOT MARMALADE
COFFEE

MONTEREY LIMAS

1 medium-sized onion, peeled and chopped
1 tablespoon butter or margarine
1 can (8-ounce) tomato sauce
½ cup sour cream
1 teaspoon chili powder
½ teaspoon salt
⅛ teaspoon orégano
3 cups cooked large California dried Lima beans
(1 cup before cooking)
1 cup diced American cheese

Cook onion slowly in butter or margarine until transparent. Stir in tomato sauce, sour cream, chili powder, salt, and orégano. Drain beans; arrange layers of beans, cheese, and sauce in greased baking dish (one and one-half quart). Bake in moderate oven (350° F.) about forty-five minutes. 6 servings.

A simple dish of good flavor and quality.

MENU

ORANGE, RAISIN, APPLE FRUIT CUP
MONTEREY LIMAS
WHOLE-WHEAT BREAD
BLACKBERRY PIE
COFFEE

BEEF-AND-BREAD CASSEROLE

½ pound ground beef
1 tablespoon butter or margarine
1 cup sifted all-purpose flour
1 tablespoon baking powder
¾ teaspoon salt
1 cup yellow corn meal
⅛ teaspoon each: thyme, basil, orégano
2 eggs
1 cup milk

Cook beef in butter or margarine in a hot frying pan until it loses its red color. Let cool slightly. Sift flour, baking powder, and salt together; stir corn meal and herbs into flour mixture. Beat eggs and add with milk. Mix all together to form smooth batter. Add meat and the fat from the pan. Pour into a greased baking dish (nine-inch). Bake in hot oven (425° F.) twenty minutes, or until well browned. Serve warm, with or without gravy. 4 servings.

Ground leftover chicken or fish delicious substitutes for beef.

MENU

VEGETABLE JUICE COCKTAIL
BEEF-AND-BREAD CASSEROLE
PEAS-AND-CARROTS
CANNED BING CHERRIES BROWNIES
TEA OR COFFEE

BEEF MIROTON

8 serving-sized slices boiled or roast beef
2 small onions, peeled and chopped
2 tablespoons butter or margarine
1 tablespoon flour
1 cup bouillon or stock
½ cup canned tomatoes
½ teaspoon salt
¼ teaspoon pepper
½ teaspoon dry mustard
1 teaspoon prepared horse-radish
1 tablespoon red-wine vinegar
2 small sour pickles, sliced thin
1 teaspoon chopped parsley

Place meat in buttered baking dish. Cook onions in butter or margarine in a saucepan until tender. Stir flour in; add bouillon or stock, tomatoes, salt, and pepper; cook and stir until boiling. Reduce heat and cook slowly twenty minutes. Remove from heat. Stir mustard, horse-radish, vinegar, and pickles into hot sauce. Pour over meat. Cover and set in moderately-low oven (300° F.) five or ten minutes before serving. Sprinkle parsley on top and serve. 4 servings.

French cooks sometimes serve baked or fried eggplant with this.

MENU

MELON-BALL FRUIT CUP
BEEF MIROTON
SCALLOPED POTATOES
BROWN-AND-SERVE ROLLS PEACH JAM
COFFEE

CALIFORNIA BAKED CAULIFLOWER

1 medium-sized cauliflower
1½ cups medium white sauce
⅓ cup coarse cracker crumbs
¼ cup chopped almonds
3 tablespoons butter or margarine, melted
½ teaspoon paprika

Wash cauliflower, remove leaves, cut off heavy stem. Turn cauliflower upside down in cold water and let stand twenty minutes. Drain. Cook in boiling salted water to cover about twenty minutes or until tender. Drain. Place in buttered deep baking dish. Pour white sauce over cauliflower. Combine crumbs, almonds, and butter or margarine, and spoon over top of vegetable. Sprinkle with paprika. Bake in moderately-hot oven (400° F.) twenty minutes, or until bubbly and browning. 4 servings.

Just as good when chopped cashews or pecans are used.

MENU

CALIFORNIA BAKED CAULIFLOWER
GRILLED HAM SLICE
DATE MUFFINS   BLUEBERRY JAM
BROILED SHERRIED GRAPEFRUIT
COFFEE

CORN-AND-MEAT PIE

1 can (20-ounce) kernel corn, or
  2 cups fresh sweet corn
2 tablespoons butter or shortening
4 tablespoons sugar
1 teaspoon salt
½ teaspoon pepper
1 cup ground cooked meat
1 medium-sized onion, peeled and chopped
¼ cup meat stock or bouillon
¼ cup seedless raisins, soaked
10 olives, sliced
2 hard-cooked eggs, sliced

Drain corn; sauté five minutes in butter or shortening with two tablespoons sugar, and the salt and pepper. Mix meat, onion, stock or bouillon, drained raisins, and the olives. Place in buttered baking dish (one and one-half quart). Arrange sliced eggs on top; season eggs lightly. Pour corn over. Sprinkle with remaining sugar. Brown in moderate oven (350° F.) fifteen minutes.

Chilean in origin; native cooks use fresh sweet corn.

MENU

CORN-AND-MEAT PIE
POPOVERS CHERRY JAM
SAUTERNES
GINGER-TOPPED PEAR COMPOTE*
COFFEE

CORN-AND-ONION SUPPER

1 can (3½-ounce) French-fried onions
1 can (12-ounce) cream-style corn
1 teaspoon salt
½ teaspoon pepper
¼ cup canned tomato sauce
1 tablespoon chopped parsley
1 can (12-ounce) whole kernel corn

Empty half of fried onions into a greased flameproof casserole (one-quart). Stir over heat just long enough to heat onions. Remove from heat and pour cream-style corn on top of onions; season with salt and pepper; cover with tomato sauce; add parsley. Make top layer of drained kernel corn. Spread remaining French-fried onions on top. Place in hot oven (425° F.) twenty minutes, until bubbly and onions browned. 4 or 5 servings.

Quickie from the pantry shelf. And delicious!

MENU

CORN-AND-ONION SUPPER
TOSSED GREEN SALAD
ITALIAN HAM SALAMI
CRACKED-WHEAT BREAD BUTTER
BEL PAESE CHEESE TOASTED CRACKERS
COFFEE

EASY CORN SOUFFLÉ

1 tablespoon butter or margarine
2 tablespoons flour
1 cup top milk
2 eggs
1 can (20-ounce) cream-style corn
1 teaspoon salt
¼ teaspoon pepper
Paprika

Mix butter or margarine and flour in small saucepan, over moderate heat; add milk gradually; cook, stirring constantly, until smooth and creamy. Beat egg yolks until light, add white sauce slowly to yolks. Whip egg whites stiff. Add corn, salt, and pepper to yolk mixture; fold in whites; pour into greased casserole (one-quart) and set in shallow pan of hot water. Sprinkle top with paprika. Bake in moderate oven (350° F.) forty-five minutes. Serve at once. 4 servings.

The best garnish is crisp bacon curls and fresh parsley.

MENU

EASY CORN SOUFFLÉ
CRISP BACON
ORANGE BREAD BUTTER
APPLESAUCE NUT COOKIES
TEA OR COFFEE

SPOON BREAD

1 cup yellow corn meal
1 cup boiling water
1 teaspoon salt
1½ teaspoons sugar
¼ cup melted shortening
1 cup milk
2 eggs
1 cup sifted all-purpose flour
2 teaspoons baking powder

Sift corn meal; stir into boiling water; add salt, sugar, shortening, and milk, and mix well. Let cool slightly. Beat eggs. Add alternately with the flour, which has been sifted with the baking powder. Beat well. Pour into a well-buttered baking dish (one-quart). Set in shallow pan of water. Bake in moderate oven (375° F.) forty-five minutes. Serve hot. 6 servings.

Nothing better for a cold night or a frosty morning.

MENU

SPOON BREAD
HAMBURGERS
CATSUP PICKLE RELISH MUSTARD PICKLE
TOASTED HAMBURGER BUNS
ORANGE-FROSTED DOUGHNUTS
COFFEE

THURSDAY NIGHT CORNED BEEF

1 cup medium white sauce
2 cups cubed leftover corned beef
¾ cup coarse bread crumbs
2 tablespoons butter or margarine
1½ cups chopped cooked cabbage
¼ teaspoon paprika
⅛ teaspoon celery salt

Combine white sauce and corned beef. Stir crumbs into melted butter or margarine. Pour half the crumbs into a greased baking dish (one and one-half quart). Spread cabbage on crumbs; pour creamed corn beef on top. Season with paprika and celery salt. Sprinkle remaining crumbs over all. Bake in moderately-hot oven (400° F.) thirty minutes, or until bubbly and browning. 4 servings.

Bake any leftover in scallop shells next day for luncheon.

MENU

HOT CONSOMMÉ MADRILÈNE
CORN STICKS
THURSDAY NIGHT CORNED BEEF
FRENCH-FRIED ONIONS (CANNED OR QUICK-FROZEN)
BRANDIED FRUIT CUSTARD*
COFFEE

ITALIAN EGGPLANT PARMIGIANA

1 pound ground beef
1 clove garlic, peeled and chopped
3 tablespoons olive oil
¼ cup tomato paste
1 can (16-ounce) tomatoes
1 cup bouillon or hot water
Salt
¼ teaspoon pepper
2 small or medium-sized eggplant
2 eggs
½ cup bread crumbs
½ pound Mozzarella cheese
½ cup grated Parmesan cheese
½ teaspoon orégano
¼ teaspoon basil

Cook beef and garlic in one tablespoon olive oil in a heavy saucepan ten minutes or until meat is cooked. Stir with fork for even browning. Add tomato paste, tomatoes, bouillon or hot water, two teaspoons salt, and the pepper. Stir to mix; cook slowly twenty-five minutes.

Wash eggplant; pare and slice. Sprinkle with a little salt. Beat eggs; dip slices in eggs, then in crumbs. Brown in one tablespoon olive oil about three minutes on each side. Place layer of eggplant in an oiled casserole (two-quart). Cover with thin slices Mozzarella cheese, meat sauce, and Parmesan cheese. Repeat layers. Bake in moderate oven (325° F.) twenty-five minutes; sprinkle top with herbs; bake another five to ten minutes. 6 servings.

So satisfying in flavor. Popular as buffet-supper dish, too.

MENU

CELERY HEARTS CARROT STICKS
ITALIAN EGGPLANT PARMIGIANA
CHIANTI
BROWN-AND-SERVE FRENCH BREAD
FRESH FRUIT BOWL COFFEE

BARBECUED SWORDFISH, STEGNER

2 pounds swordfish steak
1 teaspoon Kitchen Bouquet
3 tablespoons butter or margarine, melted
½ teaspoon salt
⅛ teaspoon pepper
½ cup dry white wine
3 tablespoons lemon or lime juice

Arrange fish steaks in buttered casserole. Brush tops and sides with Kitchen Bouquet. Combine remaining ingredients and pour around fish. Bake uncovered in moderate oven (350° F.) thirty-five minutes, or until fish flakes easily. Baste with sauce in the dish every ten minutes. 4 or 5 servings.

Other fish steaks equally good cooked in this easy way.

MENU

TOMATO JUICE PAPRIKA CRACKERS
BARBECUED SWORDFISH, STEGNER
CHABLIS
BUTTERED ZUCCHINI
CHEESE BREAD BUTTER
APPLESAUCE CHOCOLATE COOKIES
COFFEE

EASY HAM SOUFFLÉ

½ cup milk
½ cup bread crumbs
3 eggs
2 cups chopped or coarsely-ground cooked ham
(about ½ pound)
1 teaspoon salt (unless ham is very salty)
¼ teaspoon pepper
1 tablespoon minced green pepper
1 tablespoon lemon juice

Heat milk; pour over crumbs and let soak five minutes. Beat in egg yolks, one at a time. Add ham and seasoning, green pepper, and lemon juice; mix well. Whip egg whites stiff; fold into ham mixture. Turn into buttered eight-inch baking dish. Set dish in shallow pan of water. Bake in moderate oven (375° F.) forty minutes, or until puffed and delicately browned. Serve at once. 4 servings.

Good with leftover gravy or well-seasoned cream sauce.

MENU

EASY HAM SOUFFLÉ
ASSORTED CHEESES
(OKA, CANADIAN WHITE CHEDDAR, SWISS)
BUTTERED ROLLS
CHUTNEY RAISIN-AND-NUT JAM
COFFEE

FRENCH HASH

2 cups chopped leftover beef
3 large potatoes, boiled and chopped
1 large onion, peeled and chopped
2 tablespoons butter or margarine
1 egg
1 teaspoon chopped chives
¼ teaspoon marjoram
1 teaspoon salt
½ teaspoon freshly-ground pepper
½ cup flour
3 tablespoons melted beef or veal fat
¼ cup bouillon or stock

Combine beef and potatoes. Sauté onion in butter or margarine five minutes, or until onion is tender. Mix with meat and potatoes. Beat egg; add to meat with chives, marjoram, salt, and pepper. Mix thoroughly. Shape in small oblong cakes; dip in flour. Heat fat in flameproof baking dish, and brown cakes on both sides. Add bouillon or stock to dish. Braise in moderate oven (375° F.) ten or fifteen minutes. Serve with or without gravy. 4 to 6 servings.

A good red wine adds to the enjoyment of this hash.

MENU

BAKED GRAPEFRUIT
FRENCH HASH
CLARET
PICKLE RELISH   RIPE OLIVES
BAKED TOMATOES
FRENCH BREAD   BUTTER
MOCHA SOUFFLÉ*
COFFEE

LAMB VEGETABLE LOAF

1 pound lamb shoulder, ground
½ cup milk
2 eggs, beaten
2 cups coarse bread crumbs
1 teaspoon salt
½ teaspoon pepper
3 sprigs water cress, chopped fine
1 cup drained cooked peas
1 tablespoon butter

Combine all ingredients but butter in a bowl; mix lightly. Pour into greased loaf baking dish. Spread butter on top. Bake in moderate oven (350° F.) one hour, or until browned, and meat is done. Serve sliced, hot or cold, with or without tomato sauce. 4 to 6 servings.

Leftover loaf makes good sandwich filling for lunch boxes.

MENU

LAMB VEGETABLE LOAF
BAKED POTATOES
BUTTERED RYE-BREAD TOAST
MELON BALLS
SUGARED PECANS CREAM MINTS
COFFEE

ROAST LAMB ORÉGANO

8 thin slices leftover roast lamb
2 bouillon cubes
1 cup boiling water
1 teaspoon orégano

Place lamb in small baking dish. Dissolve bouillon cubes in boiling water. Add herb. Pour over lamb. Let simmer in hot oven (where dessert is baking) fifteen to twenty-five minutes, until lamb has soaked up most of the bouillon. 4 servings.

A delicious and different leftover dish for low-cost dinner.

MENU

CREAM OF TOMATO SOUP
CHEESE CRACKERS
ROAST LAMB ORÉGANO
HASH-BROWNED POTATOES
READY-MIX GINGERBREAD
COFFEE

MACARONI AND FRANKFURTERS

3 cups ziti or shell macaroni
1½ cups grated Cheddar cheese
2½ cups milk
1 teaspoon salt
½ teaspoon dry mustard
¼ teaspoon pepper
2 tablespoons tomato sauce
4 frankfurters
1 tablespoon butter or margarine
3 tablespoons buttered crumbs
Paprika

Cook macaroni in boiling salted water until tender, about twenty minutes; drain. Rinse with cold water; drain. Melt the cheese in the upper part of a double boiler over hot water; stir in milk, seasonings, and tomato sauce. Skin and slice frankfurters; sauté five minutes in butter or margarine. Arrange alternate layers of macaroni, frankfurters, and sauce in a baking dish (one and one-half quart). Make top layer sauce; cover with crumbs. Sprinkle lightly with paprika. Bake in a moderate oven (375° F.) twenty-five minutes, or until lightly browned. 4 or 5 servings.

Also a buffet favorite for teen-agers and grownups.

MENU

MACARONI AND FRANKFURTERS
RIBBON SANDWICHES
WALNUTS SMALL HOT MINCE TARTS APPLES
MILK COFFEE

BLEECKER STREET MACARONI

½ pound macaroni shells
7 tablespoons butter or margarine
3 tablespoons flour
1½ teaspoons salt
¼ teaspoon black pepper
¾ teaspoon dry mustard
1 teaspoon paprika
2½ cups milk
¼ pound Caciocavallo or milder Mozzarella cheese, grated
1½ teaspoons Worcestershire sauce
1 cup crumbs

Cook macaroni in boiling salted water fifteen minutes, or until tender. Drain; place in buttered shallow baking dish (one and one-half quart). Melt four tablespoons butter or margarine; stir in flour, salt, pepper, mustard, and one-half teaspoon paprika. Add milk slowly, stirring constantly over low heat until mixture thickens and boils three minutes. Add cheese and Worcestershire; remove from heat; stir to melt cheese. Pour over macaroni. Melt remaining three tablesoons butter or margarine, and stir crumbs in until lightly browned. Sprinkle over macaroni with remaining one-half teaspoon paprika. Bake in moderately-hot oven (400° F.) twenty-five minutes, or until browned. 4 servings.

Or substitute sharp Cheddar for the Italian cheese.

MENU

BLEECKER STREET MACARONI
SALAD OF ARTICHOKE HEARTS, CHICORY, GREEN PEPPERS, AND ANCHOVY FILLETS RED-WINE FRENCH DRESSING
RED PLUM TART
ESPRESSO COFFEE BENEDICTINE

FAMILY MACARONI

1 box (8-ounce) macaroni
1 medium-sized onion, peeled and chopped
2 tablespoons butter or margarine
½ cup bouillon or hot water
1 medium-sized green pepper, chopped
1 can (20-ounce) tomatoes
1 can (6-ounce) tomato paste
1 tablespoon chopped parsley
1 teaspoon salt
¼ teaspoon pepper
¾ pound sharp cheese

Break macaroni in inch lengths; cook as described on package; drain. Place in shallow casserole (two-quart). Cook onion in butter or margarine until browned; add bouillon or hot water, and remaining ingredients except cheese. Stir and cook until boiling. Pour over macaroni. Cut six very thin slices of cheese. Grate the rest and stir grated cheese into macaroni. Bake in moderate oven (325° F.) one hour; cover with sliced cheese and continue baking five minutes, or until cheese melts. 4 to 6 servings.

A good luxury touch: add a small can chopped broiled mushrooms.

MENU

SCALLIONS CUCUMBER STICKS
FAMILY MACARONI
WHOLE-WHEAT BREAD CHERRY JAM
WATERMELON OR CANNED APRICOTS
COFFEE

BAKED ITALIAN MEAT BALLS

1 pound ground beef
¼ cup red wine
¾ teaspoon salt
1 egg
2 tablespoons milk
1 teaspoon dry mustard
¼ teaspoon pepper
⅓ cup bread crumbs
½ cup grated Parmesan cheese
2 tablespoons olive oil
1 can (8-ounce) tomato sauce

Mix beef and wine; add salt; shape in balls. Beat egg; mix with milk and seasonings. Dip meat balls in egg mixture, then in crumbs, then in half of the cheese. Sauté in hot oil in flameproof baking dish seven minutes, or until browned on all sides. Sprinkle remaining cheese on top. Bake in hot oven (425° F.) fifteen minutes, or until meat is done. Serve hot with hot tomato sauce. 4 servings.

Chopped pimiento or chives may be added to this mixture.

MENU

BLACK BEAN SOUP WITH LEMON SLICE
BAKED ITALIAN MEAT BALLS
ITALIAN BREAD STICKS
SPUMONI
TEA OR COFFEE

MONDAY MEAT PIE

Biscuit dough, or quick-frozen biscuits for 6
1 package quick-frozen peas-and-carrots
1 cup liquid from vegetables
½ cup bouillon
½ cup leftover gravy
½ cup thin white sauce
Salt and pepper
6 small white onions, peeled and cooked
2 tablespoons chopped parsley
2½ cups cubed leftover roast lamb, veal, or beef

Mix biscuit dough and chill it. Cook peas-and-carrots as directed on package. Drain, saving liquid. Combine liquid from vegetables with bouillon, gravy, and white sauce. Add salt and pepper as needed. Add vegetables and meat, and heat together. Roll out dough and cut in rounds (or use a container of quick-frozen biscuits). Place biscuits on baking sheet, and bake in a hot oven (450° F.) fifteen minutes, or until lightly browned. Pour meat mixture into a baking dish (one and one-half quart). Sprinkle with parsley; arrange biscuits on top. Place casserole in the oven eight minutes. Serve at once. 6 servings.

When pastry top is used, bake at 475° F. until browned.

MENU

MONDAY MEAT PIE
BURGUNDY
ROQUEFORT OR GORGONZOLA CHEESE
THIN STRIPS TOASTED ITALIAN BREAD
(SEASONED WITH OLIVE OIL AND SALT)
FRESH FRUIT OR MELON
COFFEE

SWEDISH MEAT BALLS

2 slices bread, crumbed
1½ pounds ground beef
1 teaspoon salt
½ teaspoon pepper
¾ cup milk
½ cup beer
1 egg
1 large onion, peeled and chopped
1 tablespoon sugar
¼ teaspoon nutmeg
⅛ teaspoon ground allspice
¼ cup butter or margarine
2 cups bouillon
Parsley

Mix crumbs with beef, salt, and pepper. Moisten with milk and beer, using only enough liquid to make soft mixture. Beat egg, and add with onion, sugar, and spices. Shape in balls. Brown on all sides in butter or margarine in flameproof baking dish (one and one-half quart). Add bouillon, cover dish. Bake in moderate oven (375° F.) thirty minutes. Baste frequently with bouillon in dish; add more bouillon if needed. Garnish with parsley. 6 servings.

Fresh, good flavor in these oven-cooked meat balls.

MENU

SWEDISH MEAT BALLS
BEER
CUCUMBER AND TOMATO-ASPIC SALAD
CORN BREAD BUTTER
SWEDISH APPLE CAKE
COFFEE

MONDAY NIGHT PEPPERS

4 large green peppers
¾ cup canned kidney beans
¾ cup cooked Lima beans
1 small onion, peeled and chopped fine
2 tablespoons chili sauce
1 tablespoon cut chives
1 teaspoon salt
½ teaspoon pepper
2 tablespoons butter or margarine

Wash peppers, cut off tops, remove seeds. Cook in boiling water six minutes; drain. Combine drained beans, onion, chili sauce, chives, salt, and pepper. Fill pepper shells. Dot tops with butter or margarine. Place in baking dish with two tablespoons water in the bottom. Bake in moderate oven (350° F.) twenty-five minutes, until peppers are tender. 4 servings.

Especially good with leftover Sunday roast.

MENU

MONDAY NIGHT PEPPERS
SLICED COLD BEEF PREPARED MUSTARD
SPOON BREAD*
PEACH PIE COFFEE

EASY POTATO SOUFFLÉ

5 cups hot mashed potatoes
(6 medium-sized potatoes)
3 tablespoons butter or margarine
⅓ cup hot milk
1 teaspoon salt
¼ teaspoon white pepper
2 tablespoons minced peeled onion, or chives
3 egg whites
¼ cup grated Cheddar cheese
Paprika

Beat potatoes with butter or margarine, milk, salt, pepper, and onion or chives. Beat egg whites stiff and fold in. Pour into buttered baking dish (one and one-half quart). Sprinkle with cheese and paprika. Bake in hot oven (475° F.) ten minutes until lightly browned. 6 servings.

Delicious with fish; or as Lenten main dish.

MENU

EASY POTATO SOUFFLÉ
CODFISH BALLS CHILI SAUCE
BROWN-AND-SERVE CLOVER ROLLS BUTTER
DANISH APPLESAUCE DESSERT*
COFFEE

BEEF AND POTATO-STICK CASSEROLE

2 cans (8-ounce) tomato sauce
2 pounds ground beef
4 slices bread
1 egg
2 teaspoons salt
½ teaspoon pepper
1 tablespoon prepared mustard
1 tablespoon Worcestershire sauce
2 cups cooked or canned mixed green vegetables
1 can (2¼-ounce) potato sticks

Combine one can tomato sauce with meat. Crumble bread; add to meat mixture with egg, salt, pepper, mustard, and Worcestershire. Mix well. Stir in drained vegetables. Pour remaining can of tomato sauce into greased baking dish (two-quart). Spread meat mixture on sauce. Bake in moderate oven (375° F.) forty-five minutes. Cover top with potato sticks. Continue baking fifteen minutes. 8 servings.

Double recipe, and bake in two casseroles for buffet supper.

MENU

CRANBERRY JUICE COCKTAIL
BEEF AND POTATO-STICK CASSEROLE
TINY HOT BISCUITS PLUM PRESERVES
LEMON CHIFFON TARTS
COFFEE

FAMILY SALMON CASSEROLE

2 cups cooked or canned salmon
1½ cups medium white sauce
Paprika
Onion salt
3 tablespoons chopped parsley
3 large boiled potatoes, peeled
½ cup Fritos or potato chips

Remove skin and bones; flake salmon; place half of the salmon in the bottom of a buttered casserole (one-quart). Cover with one-third of the white sauce. Sprinkle lightly with paprika, onion salt, and parsley. Slice potatoes thin; place one half of them on the white sauce. Top with salmon and potatoes; cover with remaining white sauce. Add sprinkling of onion salt, parsley, and crumbled Fritos or potato chips. Bake in moderate oven (325° F.) thirty minutes, or until browned. 4 or 5 servings.

Costs little but tastes good. Substitute crumbs for Fritos.

MENU

FAMILY SALMON CASSEROLE
CABBAGE AND CARROT SALAD   RUSSIAN DRESSING
BOSTON BROWN BREAD   QUINCE JELLY
COFFEE

WESTERN SCALLOPED SALMON

2 cups cooked or canned salmon
½ cup ripe olives
4 tablespoons butter or margarine
¼ cup flour
1½ cups milk
½ bay leaf
½ teaspoon salt
¼ teaspoon black pepper
1 tablespoon grated peeled onion
1 tablespoon chopped parsley
2 bouillon cubes
½ cup dry bread crumbs
½ cup grated Wisconsin cheese

Remove skin and bones from salmon; flake salmon. Cut olives into large pieces. Melt butter or margarine in a saucepan and blend in flour. Add milk, seasonings, onion, parsley, and bouillon cubes. Cook and stir until thickened. Remove bay leaf. Place layer of salmon in bottom of greased baking dish (one and one-half quart). Sprinkle with olives, crumbs, and cheese; add layer of sauce. Repeat until all ingredients are used, topping casserole with crumbs and cheese. Bake in moderate oven (350° F.) thirty minutes. 5 or 6 servings.

For buffet parties, double this recipe and bake in two casseroles.

MENU

WESTERN SCALLOPED SALMON
BAKED POTATOES
WHOLE-WHEAT BREAD
STEWED CHERRIES COFFEE

SARDINE-STUFFED PEPPERS

4 green peppers
1 can (3¾-ounce) boneless sardines
1 tablespoon minced peeled onion
1¼ cups canned tomatoes
¼ cup chili sauce
1½ teaspoons prepared mustard
¾ teaspoon salt
¼ teaspoon pepper
¼ teaspoon dry mustard
1¼ cups cooked rice
4 tablespoons grated Parmesan cheese
2 tablespoons minced parsley
2 tablespoons butter

Wash peppers; cut off tops; remove seeds and fibers. Cover with boiling salted water and boil six minutes; drain. Pour oil from sardines into frying pan; add onion and cook five minutes, or until tender; add tomatoes, chili sauce, prepared mustard, and seasonings. Break up sardines with fork, and add to tomato sauce. Stir rice in and mix well. Fill pepper shells. Place in shallow greased baking dish. Add two tablespoons of water to the bottom of the dish. Sprinkle tops of peppers with cheese, and parsley; add dabs of butter. Bake uncovered in moderate oven (375° F.) thirty minutes. 4 servings.

For Shrimp-stuffed Peppers *substitute shrimp for the sardines.*

MENU

SARDINE-STUFFED PEPPERS
MADEIRA
BUTTERED ASSORTED ROLLS
BAKED COCONUT CUSTARD* COFFEE

SPAGHETTI WITH CHICKEN LIVERS

¼ cup olive oil
½ teaspoon freshly-ground black pepper
1 medium-sized onion, peeled and chopped
½ clove garlic, peeled
1 can (4-ounce) tomato paste
1½ cups boiling water
1 can (20-ounce) tomatoes, sieved
1 bay leaf
1 teaspoon salt
1 tablespoon sugar
½ teaspoon orégano
¼ teaspoon basil
1 package (8-ounce) spaghetti
6 chicken livers
2 tablespoons butter or margarine
¼ cup grated Parmesan cheese

Heat the oil in a (metal-base) flameproof casserole (two-quart). Add pepper; mash onion and garlic into oil, and sauté three minutes. Remove garlic. Mix tomato paste and water; stir into oil mixture and let boil three minutes. Add tomatoes, bay leaf, salt, and sugar, and simmer uncovered forty minutes. Add orégano and basil and continue cooking five minutes. While sauce simmers, cook spaghetti as described on package; drain. Add to sauce; mix lightly. Place in a moderate oven (350° F.) ten minutes. Chop chicken livers and sauté in butter ten minutes. Stir with cheese into spaghetti. Serve at once. 6 servings.

For Macaroni or Noodles with Chicken Livers *use the same recipe.*

MENU

SPAGHETTI WITH CHICKEN LIVERS
TOSSED GREEN SALAD TARRAGON FRENCH DRESSING
NAPOLEON SLICES (PASTRY SHOP) COFFEE

ONE-DISH SAUSAGE SUPPER

1 pound sausage
Salt and pepper
4 sweet potatoes, boiled, peeled, and sliced
4 apples, pared and sliced thick
¼ cup brown sugar
½ cup consommé or bouillon

Shape sausage in small cakes, season if needed; cook in hot pan until lightly browned, about five minutes. Place half of the potato slices in a greased baking dish (one and one-half quart); place sausage cakes on potatoes; cover with apple slices. Sprinkle apples with half of the sugar, and pour the consommé or bouillon over all. Cover; bake in moderate oven (350° F.) forty-five minutes; uncover and sprinkle with remaining sugar. Bake fifteen minutes longer. 4 or 5 servings.

An old favorite from an Ohio country kitchen.

MENU

SMALL APPETIZER SALAD (DEVILED EGG, PICKLE, AND OLIVES CHOPPED IN MAYONNAISE)
ONE-DISH SAUSAGE SUPPER
HOT CORN BREAD BUTTER
BAKED CHOCOLATE PUDDING*
COFFEE

SPANISH SAUSAGE AND LENTILS

1 pound small sausages
1 cup cooked lentils
1 small onion, peeled and sliced
½ clove garlic, peeled
1 green pepper, sliced
1½ cups canned tomatoes
Salt and pepper

Fry sausages in hot flameproof baking dish (one and one-half quarts) until lightly browned. Remove sausages and slice in bite-sized pieces. Drain off all but about two tablespoons of fat. Cook lentils slowly in remaining fat with onion, garlic, and green pepper until onion is yellow. Remove garlic. Add tomatoes, salt and pepper as needed, and sausages. Cover and cook in moderate oven (325° F.) twenty-five minutes, or until sausages are done. 4 or 5 servings.

Spanish cooks serve this dish on hot saffron rice.

MENU

SPANISH SAUSAGE AND LENTILS
SAFFRON RICE
ROMAINE, ENDIVE, GRAPEFRUIT SALAD FRENCH DRESSING
CRUSTY FRENCH ROLLS BUTTER
READY-MIX CHOCOLATE CAKE
COFFEE

BAKED SLICED TOMATOES

1 cup cracker crumbs
4 large ripe tomatoes, peeled and sliced
2 medium-sized onions, peeled and chopped fine
½ cup grated Cheddar cheese
½ teaspoon pepper
¼ cup crumbled potato chips
1 tablespoon butter or margarine, melted

Make a layer of cracker crumbs in the bottom of a buttered baking dish (one and one-half quart). Place tomato slices on the crumbs, and sprinkle generously with onions and cheese. Season lightly with pepper. Repeat layers, saving about one-fourth cup cracker crumbs for top. Combine crumbled potato chips, leftover crumbs, and melted butter or margarine and make top layer. Bake in moderate oven (350° F.) thirty minutes. Serve hot. 6 servings.

Tomatoes must be red-ripe; cheese should be tangy.

MENU

BEEF BOUILLON SOY CRACKERS
BAKED SLICED TOMATOES
HOT FISH STICKS
FRENCH BREAD SPREAD WITH BUTTER
FRUIT COMPOTE (APRICOTS, CHERRIES, PINEAPPLE, DATES)
COFFEE

TOMATOES AU GRATIN

6 ripe tomatoes
1 cup rye or whole-wheat bread crumbs
2 tablespoons butter or margarine
1 tablespoon grated onion
2 tablespoons chopped parsley
1 teaspoon salt
½ teaspoon pepper
2 egg yolks
¼ cup buttered crumbs
2 tablespoons grated cheese

Wash tomatoes; cut off tops, and scoop out centers. Press pulp through sieve. Heat one cup crumbs with butter or margarine until well coated. Combine with tomato pulp, onion, parsley, salt, pepper, and beaten yolks. Fill tomatoes; sprinkle tops with buttered crumbs and cheese. Place in shallow baking dish, with two tablespoons water in bottom. Bake in moderately-hot oven (400° F.) twenty-five to thirty minutes. 6 servings.

Good on the brunch table, too, with ham or bacon.

MENU

TOMATOES AU GRATIN
CRISP BACON
BRIOCHE BUTTER
PECAN PEARS*
COFFEE

TUNA-VEGETABLE SCALLOP

2 cans (7-ounce) tuna fish
1 small onion, peeled and chopped
1 tablespoon chopped capers
1 cup cooked broccoli, bite-sized pieces
1 cup medium white sauce
Paprika
3 tablespoons bran flakes
1 tablespoon butter

Drain tuna; save oil. Flake fish. Brown onion in oil. Add with capers to tuna. Place layer of broccoli in buttered casserole (one-quart); cover with tuna mixture. Pour white sauce over all. Sprinkle lightly with paprika. Cover top with bran flakes. Add dabs of butter. Bake in moderate oven (350° F.) twenty minutes, or until bubbly and brown. 4 servings.

Substitute any cooked leftover green vegetable for broccoli.

MENU

VEGETABLE JUICE COCKTAIL
SMOKED CHEESE CANAPÉS
TUNA-VEGETABLE SCALLOP
HOT BISCUITS
BUTTERSCOTCH PUDDING CREAM
COFFEE

BAKED TURKEY RING

1½ cups cubed cooked turkey
1 cup leftover stuffing
½ cup coarse bread crumbs
Salt and pepper
½ teaspoon orégano
½ cup leftover gravy (about)
3 tablespoons chopped almonds
2 tablespoons butter or margarine

Combine turkey, stuffing, and half of the crumbs. Season as needed with a little salt and pepper; add the orégano. Moisten to loaf consistency with gravy. Pour into buttered ring mold (one-quart). Sprinkle almonds and remaining crumbs on top; add dabs of butter. Set ring in a shallow pan of hot water. Bake in moderate oven (375° F.) forty minutes, or until browned. Turn out on warmed platter. Fill center with creamed leftover vegetables, such as onions and peas. 4 servings.

Just right for the day after Thanksgiving.

MENU

GRAPEFRUIT-AND-ORANGE FRUIT CUP
BAKED TURKEY RING
CREAMED ONIONS AND PEAS
CRANBERRY JELLY TOASTED ROLLS
PUMPKIN PIE
COFFEE

WHITE TURNIPS PARMIGIANA

6 medium-sized white turnips
Salt and pepper
¼ cup grated Parmesan cheese
Grated nutmeg
1 cup milk, or thin white sauce
3 tablespoons bread crumbs
1 tablespoon butter or margarine

Wash and pare turnips. Cook in boiling salted water twenty minutes, or until just barely tender. Drain; slice into buttered shallow baking dish (one and one-half quart) in layers. Sprinkle each layer with salt, pepper, cheese, and light dusting of nutmeg. Pour milk or white sauce over top. Cover with crumbs; add dabs of butter or margarine. Bake in moderate oven (350° F.) thirty minutes. 4 servings.

A hearty main dish for low-cost meal.

MENU

TOMATO JUICE
CRISP POTATO CHIPS AND CHEESE DIP
WHITE TURNIPS PARMIGIANA
GREEN PEPPER, ONION, AND AVOCADO SALAD FRENCH DRESSING
BRAIDED ITALIAN BREAD BUTTER
TEA OR COFFEE

MOCK CHICKEN CASSEROLE

1½ pounds boneless veal
2 cups boiling water
1½ teaspoons salt
½ pound sausage meat
⅓ cup chopped peeled onions
¼ cup flour
1 cup veal broth
1 cup evaporated milk
¾ cup sliced ripe olives
½ cup buttered bread crumbs

Wipe meat with wet cloth. Cover veal with boiling water, add one teaspoon salt, and bring to boiling. Lower heat, and cook gently one hour, or until tender. Let cool in broth. Drain, saving broth. Cut meat in bite-sized pieces. Brown sausage in hot skillet. Add onions and brown lightly; blend in flour and one-half teaspoon salt. Stir in veal broth and evaporated milk, and cook and stir until mixture boils thoroughly. Stir olives in with veal. Turn into shallow baking dish (two-quart) and top with crumbs. Bake in moderate oven (350° F.) thirty to forty-five minutes. 4 or 5 servings.

Favorite casserole supper of Peggy and L. B. Williams, of San Francisco.

MENU

MOCK CHICKEN CASSEROLE
ORANGE-NUT BREAD BUTTER
BLACK RASPBERRY SHERBET IN MERINGUE SHELLS
ICED COFFEE

VEAL CHOW MEIN

1 cup rice
2 pounds veal, ground
4 onions, peeled and sliced
3 cups sliced celery
1 cup canned bamboo shoots, drained and sliced
3 cups bouillon or hot water
4 tablespoons soy sauce
1½ teaspoons salt

Wash rice; drain. Combine all ingredients. Pour into a buttered casserole (two-quart). Cover. Bake in a moderate oven (375° F.) one hour. Uncover, and continue baking thirty minutes. 8 servings.

Chinese cooks brown the veal in peanut oil five minutes.

MENU

VEAL CHOW MEIN
WATER-CRESS SALAD ROQUEFORT DRESSING
TEA ALMOND COOKIES
TANGERINES DATES HAZLENUTS

ARMENIAN BAKED ZUCCHINI

1 pound ground lamb
1 tablespoon peanut oil
1 cup chopped peeled onions
2 eggs
⅓ cup chopped parsley
1 teaspoon salt
½ teaspoon pepper
2 pounds zucchini
2 tomatoes, peeled and sliced
1 cup bouillon or water

Stir meat into hot oil and cook five minutes. Add onions; stir and cook ten minutes. Beat eggs; add to meat with parsley, salt, and pepper. Mix well. Wash zucchini; cut lengthwise in narrow strips. Place layer of zucchini in buttered casserole (two-quart). Add layer of meat mixture; repeat layers. Cover top with sliced tomatoes. Pour bouillon or water over all. Cover and bake in moderate oven (375° F.) forty-five minutes; uncover and bake fifteen minutes longer. 4 to 6 servings.

Substitute beef, veal, or chicken for lamb in this dish.

MENU

CREAM OF CELERY SOUP
WHOLE-WHEAT CRACKERS
ARMENIAN BAKED ZUCCHINI
ITALIAN BREAD
CAMEMBERT CHEESE   BLACK GRAPES
COFFEE

ZUCCHINI WITH TOMATOES

2 medium-sized onions, peeled and sliced
3 tablespoons butter or margarine
2 pounds zucchini, sliced
1 can (20-ounce) tomatoes, sieved
1 teaspoon salt
½ teaspoon pepper
3 tablespoons grated Parmesan cheese

Cook onions in butter or margarine until yellow in flameproof casserole (one and one-half quart). Add zucchini and cook five minutes. Add tomatoes and seasonings, cover and cook ten minutes. Sprinkle with cheese. Bake uncovered in moderate oven (375° F.) fifteen minutes, or until cheese browns. 4 or 5 servings.

Delicious with fish, chicken, or as main dish.

MENU

BROILED CODFISH STEAKS
ZUCCHINI WITH TOMATOES
CRUSTY FRENCH ROLLS
COMPOTE OF SPICED PEACHES AND FIGS
POUNDCAKE COFFEE

the baking dish
on the barbecue terrace

DEVILED BAKED BEANS

2 cans (1-pound) baked beans
1 cup pickle relish
½ cup catsup
1 tablespoon prepared horse-radish
1 teaspoon dry mustard
½ teaspoon chili powder
1 teaspoon Worcestershire sauce
¼ cup brown sugar
1 tablespoon butter or margarine, melted
2 small corn muffins, crumbled

Empty one can of beans into a greased baking dish (one and one-half quart); cover beans with the relish. Combine catsup, horse-radish, mustard, chili powder, Worcestershire, and brown sugar. Spoon about one third of the mixture over the relish. Empty second can of beans on top of relish. Spread remaining seasonings on beans. Mix butter or margarine and crumbs, and cover top thickly. Bake uncovered in moderate oven (375° F.) thirty minutes, or until browned and crusty. 8 servings.

While hot, wrap heavily in newspaper and carry to picnic.

MENU

SLICED BAKED HAM AND ASSORTED CHEESES
BUTTERED BUNS
PREPARED MUSTARD
DEVILED BAKED BEANS
APPLES DATES STUFFED PRUNES
CHOCOLATE DOUGHNUTS
COLA DRINKS COFFEE GINGER ALE

WISCONSIN GREEN BEANS

2 pounds green beans, or
  2 packages quick-frozen
2 tablespoons butter or drippings
3 cups bouillon or beef stock
1 tablespoon flour
1 teaspoon sugar
1 teaspoon salt
2 tablespoons vinegar
Small piece summer savory
1 tablespoon chopped parsley

Wash beans; remove tips; break in pieces. Defrost quick-frozen variety. Place in casserole (two-quart) with butter or drippings and bouillon or stock. Cover; cook in moderate oven (375° F.) twenty-five minutes, or until almost done. Add more bouillon if necessary. When nearly done, sprinkle beans with flour, sugar, salt, and vinegar. Stir; let boil five minutes. Sprinkle with savory and parsley, and serve. 6 servings.

Especially good with barbecued meats and fowl.

MENU

BARBECUED SPARERIBS
WISCONSIN GREEN BEANS
ITALIAN BREAD BUTTER
FREEZER OF STRAWBERRY ICE CREAM
ANGEL CAKE
HOT COFFEE

CABBAGE BUDAPEST STYLE

1 medium-sized cabbage
1 cup sour cream
½ cup bread crumbs
3 tablespoons butter or margarine
Salt and black pepper
Paprika

Wash cabbage, cut in quarters, and boil in salted water twenty minutes, or until tender. Drain; place cabbage in buttered baking dish (one and one-half quart) with cut side up. Cover cabbage with sour cream, sprinkle with crumbs, and add dabs of butter or margarine. Season with salt, pepper, and lightly with paprika. Bake, uncovered, in moderate oven (375° F.) twenty-five minutes, or until brown. 4 to 6 servings.

Tastes extra good with roast or chops.

MENU

POTATO CHIPS   CHEESE DIP   TOMATO JUICE
BARBECUED SMALL CHICKENS
CABBAGE BUDAPEST STYLE
BROWN-AND-SERVE ROLLS   RAISIN JAM
STRAWBERRY SHORTCAKE
COFFEE

OVEN-BARBECUED DUCKLING

1 Long Island duckling, quartered
1 tablespoon olive oil
1 small onion, peeled and chopped
½ clove garlic, peeled and chopped
¼ cup each: honey, tomato catsup, red-wine vinegar
2 tablespoons Worcestershire sauce
½ teaspoon Kitchen Bouquet
¾ teaspoon dry mustard
¾ teaspoon salt
⅛ teaspoon marjoram
¼ teaspoon pepper
1/16 teaspoon rosemary

Wipe duckling with wet cloth. Place skin side up on rack in (metal-base) casserole. Roast uncovered in moderately-slow oven (300° F.) about one and one-half hours, until tender.

Prepare sauce while duckling roasts: Heat oil in saucepan with onion and garlic three minutes, or until onion is tender. Add remaining ingredients; stir well. Bring to boiling, stirring constantly. Lower heat and simmer five minutes.

When duckling is tender, drain fat from casserole, remove rack, and brush duckling with the sauce. Return to moderate oven (375° F.) for ten minutes. Give duck two more sauce applications with ten minute baking intervals. After last application, add any remaining sauce to the dish and continue to bake ten minutes. Serve at once. 4 servings.

Prepare Oven-Barbecued Chicken *or* Turkey *by the same recipe.*

MENU

ENDIVE, ORANGE, PINEAPPLE SALAD FRENCH DRESSING
OVEN-BARBECUED DUCKLING BAKED SWEET POTATOES CLARET
BROWN-AND-SERVE ROLLS GRUYÈRE CHEESE COFFEE

ONION-TOPPED EGGPLANT

1 medium-sized eggplant
1 teaspoon salt
½ teaspoon pepper
1 cup tomato juice
1 can (3½-ounce) French-fried onions

Wash eggplant; pare; cut in thick slices into a greased baking dish (one and one-half quart). Season lightly with salt and pepper. Pour tomato juice over. Cover; bake in moderate oven (375° F.) thirty minutes. Baste frequently with juice in dish, adding more tomato juice if needed. Uncover; continue baking fifteen minutes. Cover top with French-fried onions and bake fifteen minutes more, or until onions are crisp and hot. 6 servings.

Just right for any barbecued roast or fowl.

MENU

STUFFED CELERY SCALLIONS
BARBECUED SMALL TURKEY
ONION-TOPPED EGGPLANT
HOT CORN BREAD SPLIT AND BUTTERED
CHOCOLATE MERINGUE PIE
COFFEE

SAVORY STUFFED EGGPLANT

4 small, or
 2 medium-sized eggplant
Salt
4 tablespoons butter or margarine
1 cup coarse bread crumbs
¼ teaspoon pepper
½ teaspoon curry powder
¼ teaspoon dried marjoram
¼ cup heavy cream
1 cup cubed cooked chicken

Wash eggplant. Cut off top, and scoop out inside. Sprinkle a little salt in the shells and let stand thirty minutes. Cut pulp in cubes, season with two teaspoons salt, and let stand thirty minutes; drain. Cook cubed eggplant in a saucepan with two tablespoons butter or margarine, stirring occasionally, until vegetable is tender. Stir in half of the crumbs, mix, add pepper, curry powder, and marjoram. Stir in cream and chicken. Stuff into drained eggplant shells; cover with remaining crumbs, and dabs of butter. Place in baking dish, add three tablespoons water to the bottom of the dish. Bake in moderate oven (375° F.) thirty minutes. 4 servings.

Vary this by omitting curry, and topping with grated Parmesan cheese.

MENU

BROILED PORK CHOPS SAVORY STUFFED EGGPLANT
WHOLE-WHEAT BREAD
ASSORTMENT OF JELLIES (GRAPE, CURRANT, APPLE)
WATERMELON SHELL WITH MELON BALLS
ICED COFFEE ICED TEA

PICNIC MEAT LOAF

2 pounds ground steak
¾ cup grated carrots
½ cup chopped celery
2 potatoes, pared and chopped fine
2 onions, peeled and chopped fine
1½ teaspoons salt
¼ teaspoon pepper
½ teaspoon orégano
2 tablespoons chopped parsley
Leftover gravy or white sauce

Combine steak, vegetables, seasonings, and parsley; mix well. Moisten with gravy or white sauce just enough to hold shape. Place in loaf baking dish. Bake in moderate oven (325° F.) one and one-half hours, until meat is done and top browned. Serve sliced, hot or cold, with or without tomato sauce. 6 servings.

Travels well to a picnic. Serve on buttered buns, with mustard.

MENU

POTATO SALAD
PICNIC MEAT LOAF
DEVILED EGGS   PREPARED MUSTARD   OLIVES   PICKLES
BUTTERED BUNS
APPLE TURNOVERS
CARAMEL CUPCAKES
ICED COLA BEVERAGES
HOT COFFEE

ONIONS AU GRATIN

4 large Bermuda onions
Salt and black pepper
1 cup medium white sauce
¼ cup heavy cream or sour cream
3 tablespoons bread crumbs
Paprika

Wash onions; peel; cover with boiling salted water and boil twenty minutes. Drain; cut into quarters. Place in greased shallow baking dish (one-quart). Season with salt and pepper. Combine white sauce and cream or sour cream; pour all but one-fourth cup over onions. Mix remaining one-fourth cup sauce with crumbs and pour on top. Bake, uncovered, in moderate oven (350° F.) forty minutes, or until onions are tender and top is browned. 6 servings.

A fine dish with meat cooked outdoors.

MENU

HAMBURGERS BROILED WITH ANCHOVY BUTTER
ONIONS AU GRATIN
STUFFED TOMATO SALAD
(CUCUMBER, WATER CRESS, COTTAGE CHEESE, MAYONNAISE)
CRUSTY RYE ROLLS
BLACKBERRY ICE CREAM COCONUT CAKE
ICED COFFEE ICED TEA

HORSE-RADISH CREAMED POTATOES

8 medium-sized potatoes
2 cups thin white sauce
½ cup light cream
4 tablespoons prepared horse-radish
Paprika

Scrub potatoes; rinse, drain, and pare. Slice as thin as possible into a two-quart baking dish. Be sure white sauce is well seasoned; combine with cream and horse-radish. Pour over potatoes. Sprinkle with paprika. Cover and bake in moderate oven (375° F.) thirty minutes. Uncover dish, and bake thirty minutes uncovered. Serve very hot. 6 servings.

Perfect accompaniment for barbecued beef or a steak.

MENU

BARBECUED ROAST BEEF
HORSE-RADISH CREAMED POTATOES
ALE AND BEER
SCALLIONS CUCUMBER STICKS RADISHES
FRENCH BREAD SPREAD WITH GARLIC BUTTER
PAN OF WARM GINGERBREAD
BOWL OF CHERRIES BOWL OF STRAWBERRIES
ICED COFFEE

POTATOES EN MATELOTE

4 hot boiled potatoes
3 tablespoons butter or margarine
1½ teaspoons salt
½ teaspoon freshly-ground pepper
1 tablespoon chopped parsley
2 tablespoons chopped peeled onion
1½ tablespoons flour
¼ cup bouillon
¼ cup white wine

Peel potatoes, and slice into greased shallow baking dish (one-quart). Add dabs of butter or margarine; sprinkle with salt and pepper. Scatter parsley and onion evenly over all. Sprinkle with flour. Mix bouillon and wine and pour over all. Place in hot oven (450° F.) twenty minutes, or until browned. Serve very hot. 4 servings.

Called glamour spuds by the hostess who gave me this recipe.

MENU

GRILLED FRANKFURTERS
BARBECUE SAUCE
PICKLE RELISH PREPARED MUSTARD
FRANKFURTER BUNS
POTATOES EN MATELOTE
FROZEN STRAWBERRY-AND-WHIPPED-CREAM PIE
ICED TEA

SWEET POTATO SOUFFLÉ

1 can (29-ounce) sirup-pack sweet potatoes
¼ cup melted butter or margarine
½ teaspoon salt
2 tablespoons brown sugar
½ cup hot milk
3 eggs
1 teaspoon grated lemon peel

Start soufflé so it is done just as the spareribs come from the barbecue broiler. Drain potatoes; mash them with butter or margarine, salt, brown sugar, milk, and beaten egg yolks. Beat until light and fluffy. Fold in stiffly-beaten egg whites and lemon peel. Pour into ungreased casserole (one and one-half quart). Bake in moderate oven (375° F.) one hour, or until top is lightly browned. 6 servings.

Southern barbecue favorite especially with spareribs.

MENU

BARBECUED SPARERIBS
SWEET POTATO SOUFFLÉ
TOMATO ASPIC SALAD ON GREENS FRENCH DRESSING
BROWN-AND-SERVE CHEESE BISCUITS
BRANDIED FRUIT BOWL
(BRANDIED BLACK CHERRIES AND PEACHES WITH FRESH STRAWBERRIES)
ASSORTED COOKIES
COFFEE

BAKED ACORN SQUASH

4 small or 2 large acorn squash
2 tablespoons butter or margarine
¼ cup heavy cream
1½ teaspoons salt
½ teaspoon white pepper
2 teaspoons brown sugar

Wash squash; cut in half and remove seeds. Place in baking dish and add water to the depth of one-half inch. Season each half with dab of butter or margarine, a little cream, salt, pepper, and sugar. Bake in moderately-hot oven (400° F.) thirty-five minutes, or until tender. 4 servings.

So good with any barbecued meat.

MENU

TOSSED GREEN SALAD WITH FRENCH DRESSING
(LETTUCE, CHICORY, TOMATOES, WATER CRESS)
BARBECUED LEG OF LAMB
BAKED ACORN SQUASH
TRAY OF ASSORTED BUTTERED BREAD
(CHEESE BREAD, RAISIN, WHOLE-WHEAT)
CHERRY TARTS
ICED COFFEE FRUIT PUNCH

SAUERKRAUT BAKED WITH SOUR CREAM

2 pounds sauerkraut
1 carrot, scraped and cubed
1 small onion, peeled
½ bay leaf
1 teaspoon salt
5 peppercorns
2 whole cloves
1 cup dry white wine
1½ cups sour cream
1 tablespoon butter
Salt and pepper

Cover sauerkraut with cold water and let stand few minutes; drain. Repeat three times. Put in saucepan, cover with cold water, add vegetables, bay leaf, salt, peppercorns, and cloves. Bring to boiling, lower heat, cover pan, and simmer three hours. Drain. Pour into greased baking dish (two-quart), add wine and sour cream. Cook uncovered in moderate oven (350° F.) about fifteen minutes, or until liquid is absorbed. Add butter, and light seasoning with salt and pepper. Serve with barbecued meat or fowl. 6 to 8 servings.

Particularly good with spareribs, ham, and turkey.

MENU

BROILED HAM STEAKS   BARBECUE SAUCE
BEER
PICKLES   OLIVES   PICKLED ONIONS
SAUERKRAUT BAKED WITH SOUR CREAM
BUTTERED PUMPERNICKEL AND WHITE BREAD
DEEP-DISH APPLE PIE
CHEESE TRAY
COFFEE

SWISS BAKED SAUERKRAUT

2 pounds sauerkraut
3 tablespoons butter or margarine
2 apples, pared, cored, and quartered
⅓ cup sugar
½ cup dry white wine
1 teaspoon salt
½ teaspoon white pepper
1 quart water

Drain sauerkraut; heat in flameproof baking dish (two and one-half quart) with the butter or margarine. Add all other ingredients and bring to boiling. Cover; place in moderately-low oven (300° F.) and bake two to three hours. Juice should be absorbed. Serve with roast pork or spareribs, or carry out to the barbecue and serve with whatever is coming hot from the grill. 4 to 6 servings.

Makes a fine supper dish with hot grilled sausages.

MENU

GRILLED SAUSAGES
SWISS BAKED SAUERKRAUT
HOT CORN MUFFINS APPLE BUTTER
APRICOT UPSIDE-DOWN CAKE
COFFEE

VEGETABLE LOAF WITH OYSTERS

1 can (12-ounce) cream-style corn
1 pimiento, chopped
1 green pepper, chopped
1 small onion, peeled and chopped
½ cup cooked peas
1 teaspoon salt
½ teaspoon pepper
⅛ teaspoon celery salt
1½ cups toasted bread crumbs (about)
8 oysters, drained
½ cup corn meal
2 tablespoons butter or margarine

Combine corn, pimiento, green pepper, onion, peas, and seasonings. Add enough toasted crumbs to make good loaf texture. Place in buttered baking dish (one and one-half quart). Set dish in moderate oven (350° F.) and bake thirty minutes. Dip oysters in corn meal; sauté in hot butter or margarine in frying pan three minutes, or only until golden. Place browned oysters on vegetable loaf, sprinkle with any remaining corn meal and butter from frying pan. Bake five minutes more. 6 servings.

Tastes fine for barbecue or buffet meals.

MENU

BARBECUE-BROILED STEAK
VEGETABLE LOAF WITH OYSTERS
HOT BISCUITS CURRANT JAM
ORANGE LAYER CAKE
COFFEE

dessert comes hot from the oven

APPLE CAKE MERINGUE

3 large eating apples
1 cup sugar
1 cup water
6 squares or rounds spongecake
½ cup orange juice
½ cup orange marmalade
3 egg whites
2 tablespoons light brown sugar

Wash and pare apples. Cut in half crosswise; remove core. Cook in sirup of sugar and water twenty-five minutes, or until tender. Drain apples saving sirup. Place spongecake in shallow baking dish. Place apple half on each piece of cake. Cook remaining sirup down until slightly thickened. Combine with orange juice; pour over apples. Add tablespoon of marmalade to each apple half. Whip egg whites stiff with brown sugar. Heap on top of apples. Brown in moderately-low oven (300° F.) fifteen minutes, or until golden. Serve warm or cold. 6 servings.

Good flavor, lighter than it seems; for any season.

MENU

SMOKED TROUT CANAPÉS JACK ROSE COCKTAIL
FRENCH ONION SOUP
TOASTED FRENCH BREAD
BAKED CHICKEN BREASTS
CURRANT JELLY SPICED PLUMS
BUTTERED LIMA BEANS
APPLE CAKE MERINGUE COFFEE

APPLE-INDIAN PUDDING
(DEMETRIA TAYLOR, NEW YORK)

⅓ cup yellow corn meal
⅓ cup water
1 quart milk
½ teaspoon salt
¼ cup sugar
½ teaspoon ginger
½ teaspoon cinnamon
¼ teaspoon nutmeg
½ cup molasses
2 cups thinly-sliced pared apples

Combine corn meal and water. Scald milk in the upper part of a one and one-half quart double boiler; add corn meal; stir over low heat until thickened. Cover; cook over hot water twenty minutes. Remove from heat; stir in remaining ingredients. Pour into greased casserole (one and one-half quart). Bake in moderate oven (325° F.) two hours. Serve warm or chilled, with cream, ice cream, or hard sauce. 4 servings.

Easy on the budget; makes hungry folks happy.

MENU

CABBAGE AND GREEN PEPPER SALAD
MAYONNAISE
BAKED BEANS
CHILI SAUCE BOSTON BROWN BREAD
APPLE-INDIAN PUDDING
COFFEE

DANISH APPLESAUCE DESSERT

2 cups fine zwieback crumbs
1 teaspoon cinnamon
¼ teaspoon nutmeg
¼ teaspoon allspice
¾ cup butter or margarine
3 cups applesauce
10 candied cherries

Combine crumbs and spices; mix well. Melt butter or margarine; add crumbs; cook over low heat until golden brown. Arrange alternate layers of applesauce and crumbs in shallow nine-inch baking dish, beginning and ending with crumbs. Bake in moderate oven (325° F.) thirty minutes. Chill. Garnish with chopped candied cherries. Serve with or without whipped cream, or custard sauce. 8 to 10 servings.

Good flavor and easy to make.

MENU

SHRIMP AU GRATIN APPETIZER
BAKED VEAL CHOPS
LIMA BEANS WITH TOMATO SAUCE*
BROWN-AND-SERVE BISCUITS BUTTER
DANISH APPLESAUCE DESSERT
COFFEE

MAPLE-RICE APPLES

6 apples
½ cup cooked rice
¼ cup seedless raisins, or currants
¼ cup chopped almonds
1½ cups warm maple sirup

Wash and core apples; pare halfway down from the stem end. Place in a greased baking dish (one and one-half quart). Fill apples with rice mixed with raisins or currants, and nuts. Pour maple sirup over all. Cover and bake in moderately-hot oven (400° F.) thirty minutes. Uncover and continue baking until apples are tender, about fifteen minutes longer. Serve warm, with or without cream. 6 servings.

Vary the flavor by using dates, figs, candied orange peel, and pecans.

MENU

BAKED HAM SLICE
BAKED SWEET POTATOES IN JACKETS
SMALL CRUSTY ROLLS
MAPLE-RICE APPLES
COFFEE

APRICOTS POLONAISE

1 can (20-ounce) apricot halves
Pastry-mix for 1 crust
½ cup chopped pecans
¼ cup chopped orange peel
½ cup apricot marmalade
Apricot juice
¼ cup crushed macaroons

Drain apricots, saving liquid. Mix pastry as described on package. Add nuts and orange peel to pastry; roll out and shape to fit shallow baking dish. Fill with apricot halves, cut side up. Thin marmalade with two tablespoons juice from the can, and spread over apricots. Cover with crumbs mixed with enough juice to moisten. Bake in hot oven (425° F.) thirty-five minutes, until pastry and crumb topping are browned. 6 servings.

Sour cream, or vanilla ice cream make good additions to this.

MENU

TOMATO JUICE
MEAT LOAF AND GRAVY
CREAMED ONIONS
BROWN BREAD
APRICOTS POLONAISE
COFFEE

APRICOT RICE PUDDING

1 cup cooked rice
2 cups milk
3 eggs
¾ cup sugar
¼ teaspoon salt
2 teaspoons grated lemon peel
12 dried apricots, cooked
3 tablespoons apricot juice
3 tablespoons lemon juice

Mix rice, milk, beaten yolks, all but two tablespoons of the sugar, the salt, and lemon peel. Pour into buttered baking dish (one and one-half quart). Bake in a moderate oven (350° F.) twenty minutes. Remove from oven; cover rice with apricot halves, and spoon some of their juice over them. Whip egg whites stiff with remaining two tablespoons of sugar, and the lemon juice. Spoon on top of apricots. Set in moderately-low oven (300° F.) ten minutes, or until delicately browned. Serve hot, or very cold. 6 to 8 servings.

Filling! Just right with light luncheon or small supper.

MENU

SPLIT-PEA SOUP
TOASTED FRENCH BREAD HERB BUTTER
APRICOT RICE PUDDING
COFFEE

APRICOT SOUFFLÉ

½ cup apricot purée
(apricot baby food)
¼ cup light brown sugar
1 tablespoon orange juice
Grated peel 1 orange
4 egg whites
Granulated sugar

Mix purée, sugar, orange juice, and peel. Whip egg whites stiff. Fold fruit into whites. Pour into buttered and sugared baking dish (one-quart). Sprinkle a little sugar lightly on top. Set dish in shallow pan of hot water. Bake in moderate oven (325° F.) thirty minutes, or until puffed and lightly browned. Serve at once, with cold custard sauce flavored with Madeira or sherry. 3 or 4 servings.

Fragrant and delicate; perfect dinner dessert.

MENU

COCKTAILS CHEESE DIP
THIN SLICES RYE LOAF
BAKED BREAST OF CHICKEN
BUTTERED ASPARAGUS
HOT ROLLS SPREAD WITH HERB BUTTER
APRICOT SOUFFLÉ COFFEE

BLUEBERRY MERINGUE

2 packages (12-ounce) quick-frozen blueberries in sirup
4 squares or rounds spongecake
3 tablespoons grated orange peel
3 egg whites
2 tablespoons sugar

Defrost berries. Pour half of them into a buttered baking dish (one-quart). Lay spongecake on berries. Cover with remaining berries. Sprinkle with orange peel. Whip egg whites stiff with sugar. Cover casserole with meringue. Bake in moderately-low oven (300° F.) twenty minutes, or until meringue is golden. 4 or 5 servings.

For Strawberry Meringue *substitute quick-frozen strawberries in sirup.*

MENU

DALLAS TAMALE PIE*
LETTUCE CHUNKS FRENCH DRESSING
OVEN-TOASTED ROLLS (SPLIT, BUTTER, BAKE UNTIL TOASTED)
BLUEBERRY MERINGUE
COFFEE

BROWN-SUGAR BREAD PUDDING

5 slices bread
½ cup seedless raisins, soaked
2 tablespoons chopped candied orange peel
2 eggs
2 cups top milk
4 tablespoons butter or margarine
¼ cup light brown sugar
¾ teaspoon nutmeg
¼ teaspoon salt
1 teaspoon vanilla

Cut bread in small cubes. Place in buttered casserole (one and one-half quart). Drain raisins; add with orange peel to bread. Beat eggs lightly in saucepan; stir milk in with butter or margarine, sugar, nutmeg, salt, and vanilla. Heat slowly, stirring constantly until sugar dissolves; do not boil. Pour over bread cubes and raisins. Bake in moderate oven (350° F.) forty-five minutes, or until silver knife inserted near center comes out clean. Serve warm with cream. 4 servings.

For sweeter pudding, use cubed spongecake or cinnamon coffeecake.

MENU

BROILED SMALL TURKEY
BUTTERED YELLOW SNAP BEANS
HOT ROLLS   CURRANT JELLY
BROWN-SUGAR BREAD PUDDING
COFFEE

NEW ORLEANS BREAD PUDDING

1 cup brown sugar (packed)
¼ cup water
4 slices bread, buttered
⅓ cup dried currants, soaked
½ cup chopped pecans
2 tablespoons grated lemon peel
2 eggs
1¾ cups milk
¼ cup light cream
1 tablespoon sugar
¼ teaspoon salt
1 teaspoon vanilla

Boil brown sugar and water together five minutes, or until slightly thickened. Cut bread into inch squares. Arrange half of the bread in a buttered baking dish (one and one-half quart). Sprinkle with half of the drained currants, pecans, and lemon peel. Pour half of the brown sugar sirup over all; repeat layers of bread, currants, pecans, peel, and sirup. Beat eggs slightly, mix with milk, cream, sugar, salt, and vanilla. Pour over contents of dish. Place in a shallow pan of hot water. Bake in a moderate oven (350° F.) forty-five minutes, or until a knife blade inserted near the center comes out clean. Let cool slightly, and serve with or without cream. 6 servings.

The best of winter-night desserts.

MENU

SHERRY ASSORTED CRACKERS
BROWNED CORNED BEEF HASH
CREAMED CORN WITH GREEN PEPPER
CHEESE BISCUITS BUTTER
NEW ORLEANS BREAD PUDDING COFFEE

CHERRY-APPLE COMPOTE

3 large eating apples
1 cup canned black pitted cherries, drained
½ cup sugar
Juice 1 lemon
¼ cup cherry juice
2 tablespoons sherry or port
1 cup brown sugar (packed)
½ cup butter or margarine
1 cup sifted pastry flour

Wash, core, and pare apples. Slice very thin into baking dish (one and one-half quart). Add cherries; sprinkle with sugar; add lemon and cherry juice, and wine. Bake uncovered in moderately-hot oven (400° F.) twenty minutes. Cream brown sugar and butter or margarine together. Add flour and mix well. Pat pastry out and cut in six small rounds. When fruit has cooked twenty minutes remove casserole. Lay pastry rounds over fruit, leaving about one-half inch around edge. Return casserole to oven; bake twenty minutes, or until pastry is browned. Let cool slightly; serve warm, not hot. 6 servings.

Scrumptious with vanilla ice cream or whipped-cream topping.

MENU

LAMB STEW
(CARROTS, ONIONS, POTATOES)
HOT ROLLS
CHERRY-APPLE COMPOTE
COFFEE

SURPRISE CHERRY TART

¾ cup sugar
2½ tablespoons cornstarch
¼ teaspoon salt
1 cup sirup from sour cherries
2 tablespoons butter or margarine
1 cup canned red sour cherries, drained and pitted
1½ cups brandied black cherries, drained and pitted
Pastry-mix for 1 crust
Brown sugar

Mix sugar, cornstarch, and salt in a saucepan. Add sour cherry sirup and stir until smooth. Cook, stirring until thickened and clear. Remove from heat; add butter or margarine and sour cherries. Pour brandied cherries into bottom of eight-inch pie dish. Cover with sour-cherry mixture. Prepare pastry-mix using juice from brandied cherries as required amount of liquid. Roll pastry out to fit baking dish; prick with fork. Crimp pastry to dish. Sprinkle lightly with brown sugar. Bake in hot oven (425° F.) thirty minutes, or until pastry is browned. 6 servings.

Cheese pastry is another delicious topping for this tart.

MENU

BAKED SAUSAGES
MASHED CARROTS
RAISIN BREAD
CHILI SAUCE RED PEPPER RELISH
SURPRISE CHERRY TART
COFFEE

BAKED CHOCOLATE PUDDING

1 egg
1 cup sugar
1 cup milk
¼ teaspoon salt
2 cups sifted all-purpose flour
4 teaspoons baking powder
¼ cup melted shortening
3 squares (ounces) chocolate, melted
¼ cup chopped pistachio nuts

Beat the egg very light in a mixing bowl; add sugar slowly, beating constantly; add milk, beating as you add. Sift salt, flour, and baking powder together. Add all but one-fourth cup to milk mixture gradually, beating well. Add shortening and cooled chocolate. Stir three to five minutes until smooth. Sift in remaining flour. Pour into greased baking dish (one and one-half quart). Sprinkle top with nuts. Bake in moderate oven (350° F.) thirty-five to forty minutes. Serve warm with whipped cream. 8 servings.

For Baked Ginger Pudding *omit chocolate; add one and one-half tablespoons powdered ginger with flour.*

MENU

BROILED GRAPEFRUIT
ROAST VEAL
CREAMED SCALLIONS
ENDIVE AND WATER-CRESS SALAD FRENCH DRESSING
BAKED CHOCOLATE PUDDING
COFFEE

RUM CHOCOLATE SOUFFLÉ

2 cups milk
2 squares (ounces) chocolate
½ cup sugar
⅓ cup sifted flour
¾ teaspoon salt
2 tablespoons butter or margarine
4 eggs
1½ tablespoons rum flavoring
1 teaspoon vanilla

Heat one and one-half cups milk and the chocolate together in the upper part of a double boiler, until the chocolate is melted. Remove from heat and beat thoroughly. Mix sugar, flour, and salt together in a mixing bowl; stir in the remaining half-cup of milk; beat smooth. Add to chocolate mixture, stirring until thoroughly blended. Cook over simmering water until thickened, stirring constantly; continue cooking five to seven minutes, stirring occasionally. Remove from heat. Blend in butter or margarine; set aside to cool slightly. Beat egg yolks until thick and lemon colored; beat flavorings in. Add about three tablespoons chocolate mixture to yolks, beating well. Stir smoothly into double-boiler mixture. Whip egg whites stiff; fold chocolate mixture into whites. Pour at once into lightly-greased casserole (one and one-half quart). Set in shallow pan of hot water. Bake in moderate oven (350° F.) one hour, or until silver knife inserted near center comes out clean. Serve at once. 8 servings.

A fine ending for any dinner, winter or summer.

MENU

CHILLED MELON BALLS
EGGPLANT VEGETABLE CASSEROLE*
RHINE WINE
BREAD AND BUTTER
RUM CHOCOLATE SOUFFLÉ COFFEE

COCONUT CRUMB PUDDING

2 egg yolks
1 cup sugar
⅓ cup melted butter or margarine
1 teaspoon vanilla extract
½ teaspoon lemon extract
Grated peel 1 lemon
½ cup bread crumbs
2 cups shredded coconut
¼ cup milk

Beat yolks until light; add sugar and butter or margarine and beat well. Add flavorings, lemon peel, crumbs, and coconut. Mix well; add milk. Pour into buttered baking dish (one-quart). Set in shallow pan of hot water. Bake in moderate oven (350° F.) forty minutes. 4 servings.

Vary by using orange extract and orange peel in place of lemon.

MENU

FRUIT CUP (APPLE, BANANA, ORANGE, BLUEBERRIES)
MEAT LOAF TOMATO SAUCE
BRUSSELS SPROUTS
WHOLE-WHEAT BREAD
COCONUT CRUMB PUDDING COFFEE

BAKED COCONUT CUSTARD

4 eggs
½ cup sugar
¼ teaspoon salt
1 quart scalding-hot milk
1 teaspoon vanilla
1 cup shredded coconut

Beat eggs slightly in a large mixing bowl. Add sugar and salt, and mix well. Pour the scalding milk slowly into the eggs; stirring until the sugar is dissolved. Add vanilla and coconut. Pour into buttered baking dish (two-quart). Place in shallow pan of hot water; bake in moderate oven (325° F.) about thirty minutes, or until firm. The custard is done when a silver knife inserted near the center of the custard comes out clean. Let cool, then chill. Serve very cold. 6 to 8 servings.

Baked Caramel Custard: *omit coconut; add four tablespoons caramelized sugar to baking dish.*

MENU

SAVORY BRAISED STEAK*
DEVILED-EGG-AND-GREEN-PEPPER SALAD
HOT ROLLS
BAKED COCONUT CUSTARD
BROWN-SUGAR COOKIES COFFEE

BRANDIED FRUIT CUSTARD

1 cup cubed brandied peaches
½ cup brandied cherries, stoned
½ cup seedless raisins, soaked
4 eggs
½ cup sugar
¼ teaspoon salt
1 quart scalding-hot milk
1 teaspoon vanilla

Make layer of well-drained brandied fruit and raisins in bottom of buttered baking dish (two-quart). Beat eggs slightly in large mixing bowl; combine with sugar and salt. Pour the scalding milk slowly into the eggs stirring until sugar is dissolved. Add vanilla. Pour over fruits. Place baking dish in shallow pan of hot water. Bake in moderate oven (325° F.) about thirty minutes, or until custard is firm and silver knife inserted near the center comes out clean. Let cool; then chill. Serve very cold. 8 servings.

So good with rich, dark chocolate cake or poundcake.

MENU

HOT CONSOMMÉ ASSORTED CHEESE CRACKERS
BROILED FISH FILLETS TOMATO SAUCE
BROCCOLI WITH BUTTERED CRUMBS
RYE BREAD
BRANDIED FRUIT CUSTARD
COFFEE

DATE PISTACHIO PUDDING

½ cup sifted all-purpose flour
½ teaspoon baking powder
½ teaspoon salt
½ cup chopped pistachio nuts
1 cup sliced dates
2 eggs
1 cup brown sugar (packed)
1 cup heavy cream, whipped
½ cup sliced hazelnuts
2 tablespoons light brown sugar

Mix and sift together the flour, baking powder, and salt. Stir pistachio nuts and dates into flour mixture. Beat egg yolks well; beat in brown sugar. Stir dry ingredients in. Whip egg whites stiff; fold into yolk mixture. Pour into buttered baking dish (one-quart). Bake in moderate oven (325° F.) thirty-five minutes, or until firm in center. Serve warm with whipped cream into which hazelnuts and light brown sugar are beaten. 6 servings.

The perfect rich dessert for a simple supper.

MENU

SLICED LEFTOVER ROAST LAMB
STUFFED CELERY
THIN CURRANT JELLY SANDWICHES
DATE PISTACHIO PUDDING
COFFEE

GINGER RING DESSERT

1 package gingerbread-mix
2 cups applesauce, or
  1 cup heavy cream, whipped

Follow directions on package for mixing gingerbread. Pour batter into greased nine-inch ring mold (one and one-half quart). Bake in moderate oven (350° F.) twenty to twenty-five minutes. Let stand about ten minutes before removing from the mold. Turn out on a platter. Fill center with applesauce sprinkled with cinnamon. Or fill with whipped cream, plain or mixed with chopped nuts and candied pineapple. 8 servings.

Other ideas: Substitute chocolate or other favorite cake-mix for the gingerbread. Or serve a compote of brandied cherries and sliced peaches in a poundcake ring; or whipped cream with black walnuts, chopped prunes, and dates in a chocolate-cake ring.

And, of course, ice cream makes a perfect ring filling.

MENU

BALTIMORE DEVILED CRAB MEAT* BAKED TOMATOES
CHABLIS
CRUSTY FRENCH BREAD WITH HERB BUTTER
GINGER RING DESSERT
COFFEE

MOCHA SOUFFLÉ

½ cup sugar
¼ teaspoon salt
1 square (ounce) unsweetened chocolate cut in pieces
⅓ cup quick-cooking tapioca
1½ to 2 tablespoons instant coffee
2 cups milk
2 tablespoons butter or margarine
3 eggs
½ teaspoon vanilla

Combine sugar, salt, chocolate, tapioca, coffee, and milk in saucepan. Cook and stir over medium heat until mixture comes to boiling. Remove from heat and add butter or margarine. Let cool slightly while beating eggs. Beat yolks until thick and lemon colored; add vanilla and tapioca mixture and blend well. Beat egg whites until stiff. Fold tapioca mixture into whites. Pour into baking dish (one and one-half quart). Place in a shallow pan of hot water and bake in moderate oven (350° F.) fifty to sixty minutes, or until soufflé is firm. Serve at once, with plain or whipped cream, or custard sauce. 6 to 8 servings.

This is a never-fail recipe for beginner cooks.

MENU

CREAMED OYSTERS WITH CELERY
ASPARAGUS PARMESAN HOT BISCUITS
RHINE WINE
MOCHA SOUFFLÉ
COFFEE

BAKED STUFFED PEACHES

8 canned cling peach halves
2 tablespoons chopped candied orange peel
¼ cup chopped peanuts or pecans
¼ cup brown sugar
½ cup sherry or Marsala
¼ cup liquid from peaches

Place drained peach halves in shallow baking dish. Combine orange peel, nuts, and half the sugar. Fill peaches. Sprinkle with remaining sugar. Mix wine and canned peach liquid; pour around peaches. Bake, uncovered, in moderate oven (350° F.) twenty-five minutes. During baking, baste twice with juice in dish, adding more juice if needed. Serve warm. 4 servings.

To vary, cover the stuffed peaches with macaroon crumbs. Bake as described.

MENU

BROILED HAMBURGERS WITH CHIVE BUTTER
SCALLOPED POTATOES BUTTERED GREEN BEANS
SMALL CRESCENT ROLLS
BAKED STUFFED PEACHES
COFFEE

PEACH-AND-APPLE DESSERT

1 can (20-ounce) sliced cling peaches
4 eating apples
1 cup chopped toasted almonds
2 dozen gingersnaps, crumbled fine
½ cup peach juice
2 tablespoons butter or margarine, melted
2 tablespoons brown sugar
½ teaspoon cinnamon

Drain peaches saving juice. Wash, core, and pare apples; dice coarsely. Make alternate layers of peaches, apples, almonds, and crumbs in a buttered baking dish (two-quart) with crumbs as top layer. Mix peach juice and melted butter or margarine and pour over crumbs. Sprinkle with mixed sugar and cinnamon. Bake in a moderate oven (350° F.) one hour. Serve warm with or without cream. 8 servings.

When served with very cold sour cream, a conversation piece.

MENU

COCKTAILS BLUE-CHEESE DIP
WHOLE-WHEAT CRACKERS
OVEN-FRIED CHICKEN*
PARSLEY-BUTTERED ZUCCHINI
HOT ROLLS
PEACH-AND-APPLE DESSERT
COFFEE

PEACH GINGER PUDDING

1 package gingerbread-mix
3 large canned cling peach halves
2 tablespoons brown sugar
½ teaspoon cinnamon

Prepare gingerbread batter as described on package. Slice peach halves to make one thin layer in bottom of greased baking dish (one and one-half quart). Sprinkle peaches with mixed sugar and cinnamon. Pour batter over peaches. Bake in moderate oven (325° F.) forty-five minutes. Let cool to slightly warm. 6 servings.

Serve plain or with vanilla ice cream or dab of sour cream.

MENU

EASY HAM PIE*
ALE OR BEER
CABBAGE SALAD (CUCUMBERS, CELERY, GREEN PEPPER, MAYONNAISE)
TOASTED ENGLISH MUFFINS, BUTTERED
PEACH GINGER PUDDING
COFFEE

GINGER-TOPPED PEAR COMPOTE

1¼ cups gingersnap crumbs
½ teaspoon cinnamon
2 tablespoons brown sugar
5 tablespoons butter or margarine, melted
4 firm ripe pears
3 whole cloves
½ cup sugar
½ cup Madeira or Sauternes

Combine crumbs, cinnamon, brown sugar, and butter or margarine. Mix smoothly, shape into roll, wrap in waxed paper and chill while pears cook. Wash pears, cut in quarters, pare, and remove cores. Place in casserole (one and one-half quart); add cloves, and sprinkle with sugar. Add wine and enough water to make one-half inch liquid in dish. Cover and bake in moderate oven (375° F.) twenty minutes (thirty-five minutes for hard winter pears). Remove casserole and lay six slices of ginger pastry roll on top of the fruit. If too much juice in dish (pears vary), spoon out a little before adding pastry top. Bake, uncovered, fifteen minutes longer, or until pastry is browned. Serve warm. 4 servings.

Can be baked in individual casseroles if preferred.

MENU

CHEESE SOUFFLÉ*
BROILED CANADIAN BACON
CRUSTY ROLLS WITH HERB BUTTER
GINGER-TOPPED PEAR COMPOTE
COFFEE

PECAN PEARS

6 firm winter pears
½ cup chopped pecans
¾ cup maple sirup
1 tablespoon lemon juice

Wash pears; cut in half lengthwise; remove core and stem; do not pare. Arrange in buttered baking dish (one and one-half quart). Sprinkle with pecans. Combine maple sirup and lemon juice and pour over pears. Cover; bake in moderate oven (350° F. forty-five minutes, or until pears are tender. Serve warm with or without cream. 6 servings.

Mighty good when cold, too. Especially with a lemon cooky.

MENU

SEA-FOOD MÉLANGE*
BUTTERED TOAST
VEGETABLE SALAD
(BERMUDA ONION, RAW CAULIFLOWER, SWEET PICKLE, ARTICHOKE HEARTS)
TARRAGON FRENCH DRESSING
PECAN PEARS
COFFEE

PEARS IN RED WINE

6 firm ripe pears
1 cup red wine
1 cup sugar
1-inch cinnamon stick
¼ teaspoon clove
1-inch piece lemon peel

Wash pears. If large, cut in half, pare and core. Combine wine, sugar, cinnamon stick, clove, and lemon peel in flameproof casserole (one and one-half quart). Bring to boiling; place pears in sirup; cover casserole and cook in moderate oven (325° F.) thirty minutes, or until pears are soft. Baste frequently with juice in dish. (Hard winter pears need more cooking time.) Discard cinnamon stick and lemon peel. Serve warm, with or without cold custard. 6 servings.

Serve some of the same red wine used in cooking the pears with this dinner.

MENU

BLACK BEAN SOUP WITH LEMON SLICE
BAKED SARDINES*
HEAT-AND-SERVE POTATO STICKS
CURRANT-BRAN MUFFINS
PEARS IN RED WINE
COFFEE

PRUNE-AND-APPLE TART

1 can (16-ounce) prunes, or
  2 cups cooked prunes
2 eating apples
3 tablespoons sugar
1 teaspoon mixed cinnamon, ginger, clove
Grated peel ½ lemon
2 tablespoons brown sherry, or cognac
2 tablespoons prune juice
Pastry-mix for 1 crust
Brown sugar

Drain prunes; remove pits; pour fruit into buttered shallow baking dish. Wash, pare, and core apples; slice as thin as possible over the prunes. Sprinkle with mixed sugar and spices; add lemon peel, sherry or brandy, and prune juice. Prepare pastry according to package directions; roll out to fit baking dish; prick with fork. Crimp edge of pastry to baking dish. Sprinkle top lightly with brown sugar. Bake in hot oven (425° F.) twenty-five minutes, or until crust is golden. Serve warm, with Cheddar or Edam cheese.

Sour cream topping turns this into a lavish winter dessert.

MENU

ROAST DUCK
BUTTERED PEAS AND CARROTS
CHERRY JAM   CHUTNEY
BROWN-AND-SERVE WHOLE-WHEAT ROLLS
PRUNE-AND-APPLE TART
EDAM CHEESE   COFFEE

RASPBERRY MERINGUE PUDDING

2 cups fresh red raspberries, or
quick-frozen, defrosted and drained
½ cup apple or quince jelly
1 cup chopped toasted almonds
3 eggs
4 tablespoons powdered sugar
1 teaspoon vanilla or lemon flavoring

Mix berries, jelly, and nuts in the bottom of a buttered baking dish (one and one-half quart). Beat egg yolks with three tablespoons sugar; whip whites until stiff; fold into yolks with flavoring. Spread over fruit; sprinkle remaining tablespoon of sugar on top. Set in shallow pan of hot water; bake in moderately-low oven (300° F.) about thirty minutes, until top is delicately browned. Serve with whipped cream. 6 servings.

Use any other preferred fruit in place of raspberries.

MENU

BROILED SALMON STEAKS PARSLEY LEMON BUTTER
BUTTERED LIMA BEANS
TOMATO ASPIC SOUR CREAM CHIVE DRESSING
WHOLE-WHEAT ITALIAN BREAD
RASPBERRY MERINGUE PUDDING
COFFEE

INDEX